Praise for *After the Apoc[alypse]*

"Few critics [of the Iraq and Afghanistan Wa[r...more pen]etrating than Andrew Bacevich. . . . One can only hope that Bacevich is read and understood by a generation young enough to see through and reject those dismal elites [at America's helm]."

—*The New York Times Book Review* (Editors' Choice)

"An excoriating call for change . . . Bacevich's arguments are well-informed and stoked by a sense of moral outrage. Readers will agree that U.S. foreign policy needs a massive rethink."

—*Publishers Weekly*

"A timely, angry, deeply necessary book about the habits of mind that have damaged America, and how to change them."

—Peter Beinart, author of *The Crisis of Zionism*

"With a reputation for knowledgeable, incisive, and provocative readings of history, Bacevich delivers his latest addition to a growing body of thought-provoking work. . . . Broad in its scope yet concise, this is an important nonconformist interpretation of American history."

—*Kirkus Reviews*

"The proliferating crises of our moment have found their interpreter. In this piercing account, Andrew Bacevich explains how distinctively American attributes—from our national security state to our original sin of racism to our very self-concept as the world leader—have, in the twenty-first century, conspired to render the American people vulnerable where they live. Bacevich points the way forward in terms that Americans across party lines are likely to appreciate. Will their leaders?"

—Stephen Wertheim, author of *Tomorrow, the World: The Birth of U.S. Global Supremacy*

"*After the Apocalypse* is a welcome act of heresy . . . that drives a central point home: America has stumbled, badly, and will complete its precipitous fall unless measures are taken to radically reform its failed and flawed relationship with itself and the world. . . . A must read for any student or practitioner of American statecraft."

—Scott Ritter, former U.S. Marine Corps intelligence officer

AFTER THE APOCALYPSE

ALSO BY ANDREW BACEVICH

American Conservatism:
Reclaiming an Intellectual Tradition (editor)

The Age of Illusions:
How America Squandered Its Cold War Victory

Twilight of the American Century

America's War for the Greater Middle East: A Military History

Breach of Trust:
How Americans Failed Their Soldiers and Their Country

Washington Rules: America's Path to Permanent War

The Limits of Power: The End of American Exceptionalism

The Long War: A New History of U.S. National Security Policy
Since World War II (editor)

The New American Militarism:
How Americans Are Seduced by War

American Empire:
The Realities and Consequences of U.S. Diplomacy

The Imperial Tense:
Prospects and Problems of American Empire (editor)

AFTER
THE
APOCALYPSE

AMERICA'S ROLE IN A
WORLD TRANSFORMED

ANDREW BACEVICH

A METROPOLITAN PAPERBACK

HENRY HOLT AND COMPANY   NEW YORK

Metropolitan Books
Henry Holt and Company
Publishers since 1866
120 Broadway
New York, New York 10271
www.henryholt.com

Metropolitan Books® and m® are registered trademarks of
Macmillan Publishing Group, LLC.

Distributed in Canada by Raincoast Book Distribution Limited

The Library of Congress has cataloged the hardcover edition as follows:

Names: Bacevich, Andrew J., author.
Title: After the apocalypse : America's role in a world transformed / Andrew Bacevich.
Description: First edition. | New York : Metropolitan Books, 2021. | Includes bibliographical references and index.
Identifiers: LCCN 2021002254 (print) | LCCN 2021002255 (ebook) | ISBN 9781250795991 (hardcover) | ISBN 9781250796004 (ebook)
Subjects: LCSH: United States—Foreign relations—21st century. | World politics—21st century.
Classification: LCC JZ1480 .B334 2021 (print) | LCC JZ1480 (ebook) | DDC 327.73—dc23
LC record available at https://lccn.loc.gov/2021002254
LC ebook record available at https://lccn.loc.gov/2021002255

ISBN: 9781250839343 (trade paperback)

Our books may be purchased in bulk for promotional, educational, or business use. Please contact your local bookseller or the Macmillan Corporate and Premium Sales Department at (800) 221-7945, extension 5442, or by e-mail at MacmillanSpecialMarkets@macmillan.com.

Originally published in hardcover in 2021 by Metropolitan Books

First Metropolitan Paperbacks Edition 2022

Designed by Kelly S. Too

Printed in the United States of America

1 3 5 7 9 10 8 6 4 2

To the memory of Lonnie Adams and Doug Fitzgerald,
stalwart men of courage and character

Our war, up to the very end, was a war of old men,
or of theorists who were bogged down in errors
engendered by the faulty teaching of history.
It was saturated by the smell of decay. . . .

Marc Bloch, *Strange Defeat* (1940)

CONTENTS

A NOTE TO THE READER

Between the months of July and September 1940, Marc Bloch, distinguished French historian, citizen-soldier, and future resistance fighter destined to be murdered by the Gestapo, wrote a very short book to which he gave the title *L'étrange défaite*.[1] Earlier that spring, the German Wehrmacht had attacked France. The army in which Bloch was then serving as an over-aged staff captain disintegrated. That disintegration was the subject of Bloch's book.

For citizens of France, this disaster came as a profound shock. It just wasn't supposed to happen. France had long ranked among the world's great powers and possessed a proud military tradition. Just two decades earlier, in what was then history's costliest war, the French army prevailed over the German invader. Now, that same army collapsed in a matter of a few weeks. *L'étrange défaite* was a soldier-historian's effort to understand the roots of that catastrophe.

Published after the war in French and subsequently in

English as *Strange Defeat*, Bloch's account became an instant classic. Written in what he admitted was a "white heat of rage," his slight monograph was not an expression of dispassionate scholarship.[2] It was instead an indictment of those who had laid France open to defeat, occupation, and humiliation.

The primary explanation, he charged, was "the utter incompetence of the High Command," both military and civilian. Defeat stemmed directly from a failure of leadership.

My purpose in writing *After the Apocalypse* compares with Bloch's. In books and essays published over the past twenty years, I have called attention to various failures of American leadership, particularly related to this country's recurring misuse of military power.

In 2020, those failures came home to roost. The disaster befalling the United States that year differed from the one suffered by France eighty years earlier. Yet the ultimate explanation was similar: incompetence at the highest levels, compounded by hubris, negligence, and an inability to learn.

Like Bloch, I make no pretense of dispassion. The matters I discuss are still too close at hand and urgent to permit dispassion.

"The generation to which I belong has a bad conscience," Bloch wrote in *Strange Defeat*. With some honorable exceptions, the generation of Americans to which I belong has traded its conscience for a mess of pottage.

So I offer this book not for my own contemporaries but for those who will inherit the muddle we have made. I hope they may benefit from this reflection on what happens when decay is left unattended.

Walpole, Massachusetts
October 2020

AFTER THE APOCALYPSE

NOT SO INNOCENT

During the summer of 2020, as I was writing this book, nervous Americans sensed the onset of a terrifying Apocalypse. Wildfires scorching vast areas of California, Oregon, and Washington and hurricanes pummeling the Gulf Coast reinforced those terrors. Fears that events were literally taking an apocalyptic turn became explicit and widespread. Editors inserted the term itself into headlines. THE APOCALYPSE FEELS NIGH.[1] THE CLIMATE APOCALYPSE HAS ARRIVED.[2] HOW THE APOCALYPSE BECAME THE NEW NORMAL.[3] AN APOCALYPTIC AUGUST IN CALIFORNIA.[4] APOCALYPSE IN CALIFORNIA—COMING TO YOU SOON.[5] By implication, that *you* could be anyone anywhere.

Fires and floods were only the latest in a succession of punishments Americans were obliged to endure. First had come the toxic and divisive presidency of Donald Trump. Then in the spring of 2020, a deadly pandemic engulfed the nation, nearly bringing it to its knees. Trailing just steps behind came an economic collapse so severe as to elicit comparisons with the Great

Depression of the 1930s. Before Americans had fully absorbed these disruptions, a mass movement demanding a reckoning with the nation's legacy of racism erupted, unleashing, in turn, a white nationalist backlash.

Rancor, pestilence, want, and fury: These are the Four Horsemen comprising our own homemade Apocalypse. Each came as a shock to the system. Each exposed weakness and rot in institutions whose integrity Americans had long taken for granted. Each caught members of the nation's reigning power elite by surprise.

Trump's ascent to the White House exposed gaping flaws in the American political system, his manifest contempt for the Constitution and the rule of law placing in jeopardy our democratic traditions. The coronavirus pandemic exposed gaping flaws in the prevailing concept of national security, with Americans exposed to life-threatening perils to which government authorities responded tardily and ineffectually.[6] In a matter of weeks, the economic crisis it induced threw tens of millions out of work and drove millions of businesses into bankruptcy. As for the popular uprising known as Black Lives Matter, it exposed deep-seated and widespread residual opposition to genuine racial equality.

The calamities that accumulated during 2020 fostered a sense of things coming undone. The political order seemed unable to cope. Crises following one another in rapid succession tested Americans as they had not been tested for generations. Each crisis compounded the significance of the others. Taken together, they gave birth to a moment of profound and disturbing revelation.

What this revelation will ultimately signify remains to be seen. Perhaps post-Apocalypse America will experience a great revival, comparable to what occurred in the 1860s, when a radical realignment of national politics accelerated the nation's emergence as the world's wealthiest country, albeit only after the fiery trial of civil war. Or perhaps, as it emerges from its present trials, the United States will suffer the fate of the Third French Republic in the 1930s. Sustained political dysfunction combined with a dismally inadequate response to external danger spelled the end of France's standing among the great powers.

The premise of this book is quite simple: Regardless of whether our self-inflicted contemporary apocalypse leads to renewal or further decline, the United States will find itself obliged to revise the premises informing America's role in the world. Put simply, basic U.S. policy must change.

Even before COVID-19 swept the nation, taking hundreds of thousands of American lives, cumulative policy failures ought to have made it clear that a national security paradigm centered on military supremacy, global power projection, decades-old formal alliances, and wars that never seemed to end was at best obsolete, if not itself a principal source of self-inflicted wounds. The costs, approximating a trillion dollars annually, were too high.[7] The outcomes, ranging from disappointing to abysmal, have come nowhere near to making good on promises issued from the White House, the State Department, or the Pentagon and repeated in the echo chamber of the establishment media.

Through its own fecklessness during the 1920s and 1930s, the government of France laid the foundation for its 1940 defeat by Nazi Germany. Similarly, the fecklessness of U.S. policy during the two decades after 9/11 paved the way for the afflictions of 2020.

The terrorist attacks of September 2001 prompted Washington to double down on its commitment to military supremacy and global power projection as essential to keeping Americans safe and preserving our way of life. No alternative course received serious consideration. No debate about the prerequisites of basic national security occurred. The beating of war drums allowed no room for hesitation—or even serious reflection.

However belatedly, the Apocalypse of 2020 demands that Americans finally take stock of what post–Cold War national security policies have produced and at what cost. Nearly two decades after 9/11, we can no longer afford to postpone acknowledging our own folly. It's time to remove the blinders. This, too, describes my book's purpose: to identify the connecting tissue between the delusions of the recent past and the traumas that are their progeny.

Our Apocalypse didn't come out of nowhere. It had antecedents, evident in the very way we have packaged the past—what we have chosen to remember and what to discard, what to enshrine and what to ignore.

Sadly, however, even today that failed national security paradigm remains deeply entrenched in Washington. Its persistence testifies to the influence of the military-industrial complex, the lethargy of an officer corps that clings to demonstrably flawed conceptions of warfare, and the policing of mainstream discourse to marginalize critical voices. Enabling each of these is the pronounced apathy of the American people who, apart from ritualistic gestures intended to "support the troops," have become largely indifferent to the role this country plays in global affairs. Above all, however, a defective approach to policy survives because those charged with thinking about America's role in the world cling to a series of illusions that derive from a conveniently selective historical memory.

Entry into the precincts where insiders formulate American statecraft comes at a price. It requires individuals to forfeit or at least to suppress any inclination to genuinely independent thought. To be accepted as a member in good standing of the American political class is to pledge allegiance to a worldview. Central to that worldview is a particular conception of history and of America's designated role in bringing that history to its intended conclusion.

In 1776, Tom Paine wrote that "we have it in our power to begin the world over again." In the centuries since, Paine's disciples and imitators have claimed for the United States the prerogative not only of instituting new beginnings but of specifying ultimate destinations. Indeed, through its own evolution toward an ever "more perfect Union," America itself *embodies* history's final destination—or so members of the political class purport to believe.

All such claims fall under the heading of American Exceptionalism, a concept that stands in relation to basic U.S. policy as the Facebook motto "Bring the World Closer Together" does to the mission of that corporate behemoth. Such taglines—"Workers of the World, Unite!" and "Liberté, égalité, fraternité" offer other examples—serve as a source of legitimacy while avoiding any reference to power. Rather than describing actual purpose, they disguise it. Take such slogans seriously and you can get away with just about anything, as the United States has done for much of its history.

Nearly twenty years ago, I wrote a book called *American Empire* that took issue with the ideology of exceptionalism. As an epigraph meant to signal the book's purpose, I chose a comment that Secretary of State Madeleine Albright made on February 19, 1998, during an appearance on NBC's *Today* show. "If we have to use force," she said, "it is because we are America; we are the indispensable nation. We stand tall and we see further than other countries into the future."[8] Prompting this jaw-dropping assertion——a monument to the vainglory pervading the American ruling class, both then and now—were preparations within the administration of President Bill Clinton to target Iraq with yet another round of air strikes, deemed necessary by authorities in Washington who had persuaded themselves that Iraqi dictator Saddam Hussein posed an existential threat to the United States.

Four days after Albright spoke, the World Islamic Front proclaimed a "Jihad Against Jews and Crusaders." Co-authored by Osama bin Laden, then an obscure militant Islamist, that document identified the expulsion of U.S. forces from the Arabian Peninsula as a moral imperative requiring the support of Muslims worldwide.[9] Here beckoned the actual future, one to which Albright and other members of the foreign policy establishment would remain steadfastly oblivious until the World Trade Center collapsed in a pile of smoke, debris, and dust. The baleful train of events that ensued, notably a series of costly wars that played directly into the hands of those same jihadists, testified to the inability of that establishment either to discern the future or even deal with the present, much less position the United States as history's vanguard.

Nor was this deficiency confined to the top level of the political hierarchy. In claiming to "see further," Albright was speaking the lingua franca of American statecraft. Persons of less exalted rank than secretary of state adopted a similar patois, even if in somewhat more vulgar form.

A year after my son was killed in Iraq in May 2007, I accepted an invitation to speak at a Memorial Day event in our hometown of Walpole, Massachusetts. Rather than give a speech, I read a distinctly non-celebratory poem written by a British soldier-poet during World War I. Also appearing on the program were two local officials, the state assemblyman and the state senator who at the time represented our town. Then entering its fifth year, the Iraq War had obviously not gone well. To my astonishment those two legislators, their duties not even remotely related to military affairs, each launched into a rousing presentation that offered variations on Albright's theme: The ongoing war was a righteous one; the troops were certain to prevail; the eventual triumph of freedom and democracy was assured.

At that moment, I got an inkling of just how far the toxins of American Exceptionalism had seeped into the body politic. Soon enough I concluded that redefining the nation's role in the world will remain all but impossible until Americans themselves abandon the conceit that the United States is history's chosen agent and recognize that the officials who call the shots in Washington are no more able to gauge the destiny of humankind than their counterparts in Berlin or Baku or Beijing. Even at home, the shots they call all too often go astray, as illustrated by the federal government's belated and hapless response to the COVID-19 pandemic.

Like citizens around the world, ordinary Americans are mostly along for the ride, awaiting the next unpleasant surprise, a point the events of 2020 surely ought to have driven home. Americans don't make history, whatever speechifying members of the political class may claim; they suffer its torments and adapt to its demands.

In her address to the 2016 Democratic National Convention, Hillary Clinton declared that "America is great because America is good." It would be tempting to write off Clinton's banal and utterly predictable statement as nothing more than standard political pandering. To do so is to miss its true significance. She had, after all, played a not insignificant role in fostering the costly wars that advanced the cause of the jihadists after 9/11. As a member of the Senate, Clinton had voted in favor of President George W. Bush's illegal invasion of Iraq in 2003. As secretary of state in 2011, she had engineered an armed intervention in Libya that unleashed the forces of anarchy there. Yet in her address accepting her party's nomination as its candidate for president, she was still intent on signaling that her credentials as a true believer in American Exceptionalism were in good order—even if doing so required considerable quibbling.

Give Donald Trump credit for this much: He did not labor under the illusion that America is great because it is good. Not long after denying Clinton her all-but-assumed election victory, he sat for an interview in which he was pressed to explain his friendly attitude toward Russian dictator Vladimir Putin. "He's a killer," the interviewer charged. "There are a lot of killers," Trump responded. "You think our country's so innocent?"

Startling, distinctly unpresidential, and for Trump never to be repeated, here was a truth long deemed inadmissible among adherents of American Exceptionalism. By professing that truth, Trump had committed heresy. It was as if the pope had charged Christ's apostles with perpetrating a hoax on Easter Sunday.

The inverse of innocence is not guilt but moral awareness. This book uses Trump's admission as a point of departure. Proceeding from the premise that the United States is neither innocent nor lacking in alternatives, the chapters that follow explore how a morally aware nation facing numberless challenges at home and abroad, but still retaining considerable power and influence, could adapt itself to a rapidly changing global order.

Doing this requires first unearthing the substructure of existing U.S. policy, the seldom-examined assumptions and taken-for-granted practices that have sustained the national security apparatus and shielded its myriad activities from anything more than perfunctory oversight. So in the chapters that follow, I do not concern myself with whether to reduce nuclear arsenals, curb presidential war powers, cancel particularly pricy weapons programs, reconstitute the tradition of the citizen-soldier, or cut the Pentagon budget by some specified amount. Rather, my aim is to shed light on why such worthy proposals never receive more than cursory consideration within the closed circles where policy is debated and decisions made. In other words, I focus on underlying factors that perpetuate a patently defective status quo and prevent much-needed reform.

On that score, *After the Apocalypse* may be read as a reflection on manufactured memory. Whether related to family, race, ethnicity, religion, politics, or nation, the past is a human construct. It is not fixed but malleable, not permanent but subject to perpetual reexamination and revision. The value of history correlates with purposefulness. Changing times render obsolete the past that we know and require the discovery of a "new" history better suited to the needs of the moment.

The global order today is not what it was when I was born in 1947. Yet in Washington, basic assumptions regarding America's anointed role in history still derive from that moment of transition between epic triumph just concluded and protracted struggle only just begun. If anything, the subsequent course of the Cold War deepened World War II's hold on the American collective consciousness. Even the myriad disappointments and miscalculations of the post–Cold War decades have left the historical consciousness of 1947 remarkably intact.

Americans have much to learn from the accursed events of 2020. Not least of all they should come to understand how the history that they blindly accept as true has lost its relevance. Repositioning the United States in a radically changed global order will require a radically revised understanding of our own past. In this context, historical revisionism is not an academic exercise but a precondition of sound statecraft.

So *After the Apocalypse* examines the manufactured memory embedded in prevailing conceptions of American global leadership; the obsolescence of the "West" as a geopolitical construct; the distortions induced by "special relationships"; the consequences of preferring familiar or bureaucratically convenient threats to those that are actually pressing; the evolving significance of race in U.S. national security policy; the complexities of imperial mismanagement when denying the empire's very existence; and the policy implications of changes in the nation's collective consciousness now reaching full flood. The book closes by spelling out how an appreciation of such factors could translate into an arguably more sensible and affordable approach to national security.

Nearly twenty years have passed since the shock, horror, and humiliation of 9/11. The events of that single day ought to have discredited once and for all post–Cold War claims that God or Providence had summoned the United States to determine the future of humankind. Policy elites insisted otherwise. Intent on affirming America's place as the engine of history, they embarked upon a course of action that laid the basis for the convulsions of 2020, with ill-advised adventurism abroad allowing vulnerabilities at home to fester unattended. During that interval reckless irresponsibility defined the principal theme of American statecraft.

An alternative course remains possible, one based on realism, prudence, scrupulous self-understanding, and an appreciation of the world as it is rather than as policy elites might wish it to be. The monumental arrogance and ignorance prevailing in the inner circles of power have led Americans to misapprehend their place in the global order. *After the Apocalypse* identifies habits and delusions—some dating back decades—that account for our present confusion. In that sense, although in some respects a policy book, it is also a meditation on history and its misuse.

In order to conceive of and implement a responsible approach to statecraft, Americans will have to think anew. The need for them to do so could hardly be more urgent.

1

OLD, NEW, NEXT

In the midst of the coronavirus pandemic, Pope Francis told an interviewer, "We need to recover our memory because memory will come to our aid."[1] Such pontifical advice finds application well beyond his own flock. Recovering from the ill effects of American Exceptionalism will entail remembering things most Americans would rather forget.

The "history" that shapes our political consciousness—and therefore legitimates the use of U.S. military and economic power—consists almost entirely of selectively remembered events. And while what we choose to remember, carefully curated to remove or conceal unbecoming details, may be convenient, the results come nowhere near to offering a complete and accurate record of the past.

From the very beginning of the Trump presidency, journalists entertained themselves and their readers by tallying up the forty-fifth president's vast accumulation of half-truths, untruths, and outright lies.[2] President Trump was unquestionably a congenital dissembler. Yet when it comes to the use of U.S. power to further the nation's ambitions, Americans have long since made their peace with half-truths, untruths, and lies on a recognizably Trumpian scale.

Going back at least as far as President Andrew Jackson's expulsion of the Cherokees from their ancestral lands, dissenters have denounced this habit of official dissembling to little avail. In 1836, the chief of the Cherokee Nation wrote Congress to protest the forced eviction of his people from their lands. In an eloquent letter, Chief John Ross pleaded that "such an act of injustice and oppression" could "never knowingly be countenanced by the Government and people of the United States." Yet it *was* knowingly countenanced, with a minimum of regret that was without practical effect.

A decade later, Senator Thomas Corwin of Ohio took to the floor of the Senate to decry the ongoing U.S. war with Mexico, undertaken under a "hypocritical pretense" devised "to conceal the avarice which prompted us to covet and to seize by force that which was not ours." Corwin felt certain that eventually the truth would come out. "Whatever we may say today," he insisted, "or whatever we may write in our books, the stern tribunal of history will review it all, detect falsehood, [and] bring us to judgment." In reality, once California and the Southwest were ours, Americans wasted no time in making their peace with hypocritical pretense.

At the end of the nineteenth century, hypocritical pretense found expression even farther afield, sending Mark Twain into a fit of outrage. The annexation of the Philippine archipelago, seized in a war ostensibly undertaken to liberate Cuba, prompted him to revise the lyrics of "The Battle Hymn of the Republic."

Mine eyes have seen the orgy of the launching
   of the Sword;
He is searching out the hoardings where the
   stranger's wealth is stored;
He hath loosed his fateful lightnings, and with
   woe and death has scored;
His lust is marching on.

After killing an estimated two hundred thousand Filipinos, U.S. forces succeeded in pacifying the Philippines. Twain's ditty was soon forgotten.

I cite these distant episodes in the chronicle of American expansionism to make a larger point: Our collective capacity for misremembering (or altogether forgetting) inconvenient facts is bottomless—and plays a crucial role in sustaining American Exceptionalism. Available yet inert, such inconvenient facts may attract occasional notice and from time to time even cause twinges of remorse. (Who can feel good about the fate that Native Americans suffered at the hands of the U.S. government?) Soon enough, however, such facts get filed away under the heading of "not especially relevant," and the myth of Americans as God's new Chosen People survives with hardly a scratch. In the final analysis, only facts that sustain a belief in American Exceptionalism count.

To illustrate how this works, consider an essay that Joe Biden published in *Foreign Affairs* just as the coronavirus pandemic of 2020 began to bite.[3] Carrying the predictable title "Why America Must Lead Again," the essay conveyed the former vice president's foreign policy vision just as he was mounting his run for the White House. Although it appeared in the wake of a two-decade period during which American leadership had produced less than reassuring results, Biden did not tarry over mistakes. For example, he made absolutely no mention of the 2003 invasion of Iraq, which as chair of the Senate Foreign Relations Committee he had ardently supported.[4] Instead, the would-be commander in chief offered a something-for-everyone potpourri of promises, touching on subjects ranging from trade and climate change to fighting corruption abroad and "lifting up women and girls around the world." Prominently featured in this smorgasbord were assurances of his willingness to use force if need be and a vow that the United States would continue to possess "the strongest military in the world," as if a reluctance to employ violence or a shortfall in available striking power had somehow hampered recent U.S. policy.

Unpacking Biden's foreign policy vision requires giving due attention to the clichés trotted out to clinch his argument. History itself, he insisted, validated that vision. "This is not a moment for fear," Biden assured his readers, echoing Franklin Delano Roosevelt's First Inaugural Address, delivered in the midst of the Great Depression. "This is the time to tap the strength and audacity that took us to victory in two world wars and brought down the Iron Curtain. The triumph of democracy and liberalism over fascism and autocracy created the free world. But this contest does not just define our past. It will define our future, as well."

Here, in a nutshell, is the narrative that props up American Exceptionalism: the conviction that a succession of victories, engineered by the United States, had "created the free world," thereby weaving past, present, and future into a single seamless garment. That this narrative cannot withstand even minimally critical scrutiny is beside the point. (Does the outcome of World

War I qualify as a victory or did it pave the way for something worse? And didn't Soviet leader Josef Stalin, neither democratic nor liberal, somehow figure in defeating fascism in World War II?) Biden's framing of history excluded all that happened before 1914 and after 1989, while airbrushing more than a little of what happened in between. By depicting history as a story of America rising up to thwart distant threats, he captured the essence of the past to which establishment politicians, i.e., just about everyone except someone like Donald Trump, still instinctively revert in stump speeches or on patriotic occasions.

My late mother, a devout pro-life Catholic and proud veteran of World War II, would never have voted for Joe Biden and certainly not for Hillary Clinton, whom she despised. Yet my mother would have thoroughly approved of their take on the role that America had played in recent history. After all, she had lived that history. Nothing that she had encountered from her birth in the 1920s, through depression, global war, and Cold War, to her death not long after her grandson was killed in Iraq had caused her even a shadow of doubt. She, too, fervently believed that "America is great because America is good."

Old Order, New Order, Next Order

But are the events that defined my mother's life still pertinent? Should those events define the lives of her children's grandchildren? Or is it possible that we are now living in a completely different time? Perhaps the only good thing about our brush with the Apocalypse is that it invites us to address such questions head-on.

The late Arthur Schlesinger Jr. (1917–2007) was as much

a political operative as a prizewinning historian. His scholarly reputation rests primarily on his multipart *Age of Roosevelt*, the first volume of which, *The Crisis of the Old Order*, appeared in 1957. In Schlesinger's telling, the disappointing outcome of the European War of 1914–1918—few Americans during the 1920s and 1930s regarded it as much of a victory—when combined with the Great Depression, spelled the demise of that Old Order, which Schlesinger portrayed as suffering from terminal exhaustion.

"Fatigued with the higher idealism" that according to Schlesinger had defined the Progressive Era, Americans after the World War embraced an "ethos of normalcy." In his telling, normalcy meant conformity, complacency, and deference to "devotees of the business cult." The prevailing national mood was drab, dull, and predictable, Schlesinger comparing it to life in a sleepy midwestern town—"the shady streets, the weekly lodge meetings, golf on Sunday morning, followed by a fried chicken dinner and an afternoon nap."[5]

Beginning in 1933, as Schlesinger spins the tale, the New Deal, along with Franklin Roosevelt's inspiring leadership in a triumphal second world war, inaugurated a New Order that was vigorous, enlightened, and progressive. Schlesinger portrayed its domestic politics as pitting stodgy conservatives against forward-looking liberals. What actually distinguished his New Order was a sublime ideological clarity: An era defined internationally by conflicts pitting democratic capitalism against various forms of totalitarianism was all about choosing sides. The New Order did not encourage doubts.

Much as FDR played a key role in creating that order, it fell to Cold War presidents from Harry Truman to Ronald Reagan to sustain it. Not all of them enjoyed equal success in doing so.

Yet leading the "free world" defined the standard by which all were judged.

Even after the fall of the Berlin Wall in 1989, that standard remained intact. During the post–Cold War era, Presidents Bill Clinton, George W. Bush, and Barack Obama all sought to keep the New Order alive, even if from time to time that meant putting it on a figurative ventilator. Despite a long train of shocks, including the bursting of the 1998 dot-com bubble, a court-brokered presidential election in 2000, the 9/11 attacks, the futile Global War on Terrorism, the devastation inflicted by Hurricane Katrina in 2005, and the Great Recession of 2007–2008, not to mention the rise of Donald Trump, political elites clung to their belief in the New Order. Across America, once-preeminent denominations of mainline Protestantism might be in a tailspin, but in Washington faith that God had singled out the United States as his instrument of salvation remained fixed in place.[6]

That the parable Schlesinger had conjured up (its essentials affirmed by countless other writers since) hovers in the background of Biden's *Foreign Affairs* essay of 2020 is then hardly surprising. Even as I write this, the American political establishment (Donald Trump himself always excluded) clings to the illusion that in some cosmic sense the moral and geopolitical outlook to which most Americans implicitly subscribed between 1945 and 1989 remains fully relevant. Within days of his election to the presidency, Biden himself was assuring foreign leaders that "America is back."[7]

That the conditions imparting to that period its characteristic vibe have long since vanished somehow manages to escape notice. Belief that the United States is still charged with leading a "free world" against the forces of darkness lingers.

At the outset of the post–World War II era, with most of Europe and much of Asia laid waste and the United States undamaged and all but self-sufficient, American economic and technological supremacy was indisputable. Sole possession of nuclear weapons guaranteed U.S. military preeminence as well. The shattered and demoralized nations of Western Europe desperately needed American aid and protection. Even the former Axis powers, Germany, Italy, and Japan, looked to Washington for assistance. In the Far East, China was weak and poised on the brink of civil war. Only the Soviet Union held out against the near-global postwar Pax Americana, intent on exporting an ideological alternative to liberalism and building its own empire.

Those were the circumstances that vaulted the United States to a position of unparalleled global preeminence. By 1989, not a single one of them remained. By then, however, the conviction that preeminence had become an American birthright had long since taken root in Washington.

The fall of the Berlin Wall, an event occasioning great celebration but minimal reflection, seemingly ratified the exertions and sacrifices of the previous several decades. With the passing of the Cold War, an opportunity to create a bigger and better Pax Americana presented itself. After decades of conflict and competition, only a single superpower remained. Assertive U.S. global leadership was therefore more important than ever. That the nation possessed the wherewithal to fulfill that role was a given. No conceivable alternative existed.

Much like Arthur Schlesinger's Old Order in 1932, however, the New Order was running on fumes. The evidence was everywhere—in appalling economic inequality, seemingly intractable racism, social disintegration, mushrooming personal indebtedness, budget deficits, trade imbalances, and above all a loss of faith in the American system.[8] For a nation deeply committed to remaining the world's leading military power, especially telling was the disparity between the munificent resources funneled to the Pentagon and the largely ruinous results actually achieved by U.S. interventions abroad, which became more frequent and more expensive as the Cold War receded into the past.

Put to the test, the assumptions underlying post–Cold War expectations of the United States continuing to exercise global leadership and thereby defining the future—the outlook expressed by Madeleine Albright—did not hold up. Yet much as Detroit kept right on calling itself the Motor City even while bleeding market share to European and Japanese automakers, Washington remained in deep denial.

In that regard, the election of 2016 mirrored the election of 1932: Rather than nursing the status quo any further, the voters who installed Donald Trump in the Oval Office were counting on him to chart a new course. In truth, neither Roosevelt nor Trump possessed a clear understanding of where such a new course might lead. Both presidents flew by the seat of their pants. As Inauguration Day 1933 approached, Schlesinger wrote, FDR was "calm and inscrutable, confident that American improvisation could meet the future on its own terms."[9] Calm was never Trump's MO, but improvisation bordering on whimsy was to become a signature of his administration.

What the troubles that swept across the American landscape during the summer of 2020 made unmistakably clear, however, was that further improvisation wouldn't do. Trump's presidency signified the final demise of the New Order. As to what should replace it, he was plainly clueless. Candidate Biden's attempt to finesse the question by vowing to restore America's position as leader of the "free world" possessed about as much relevance as President Trump's own mid–February 2020 assurances that with the advent of warmer weather COVID-19 was sure to disappear.[10]

Like it or not, that Next Order is upon us. Identifying its parameters can no longer be postponed—and that means having done with American Exceptionalism once and for all.

History for the Next Order

To facilitate a timely transition to that Next Order, Americans should heed the counsel of Pope Francis and recover their memory. At least with regard to race, the events of 2020 did prompt such a recovery: A seemingly endless series of incidents in which police officers killed Black citizens provoked widespread outrage that transcended racial lines. As a direct consequence, many Americans—by no means all—rediscovered racism. As never before, "white privilege" now emerged as a seemingly indelible stain on the nation's soul.

In the realm of international politics, the counterpart of "white privilege" is "American privilege." In common with other Great Powers past and present, the United States habitually asserts the prerogative of judging its behavior on the global stage in accordance with its own preferred and eminently flexible standards.

Just as the self-congratulatory domestic narrative centers on the ineluctable expansion of freedom "from sea to shining sea," so, too, the narrative of America abroad emphasizes the spread of freedom to the far corners of the earth. The heroic narrative of America abroad is even less inclined than the domestic narrative to allow room for ambiguity and paradox. Hence, the exclusion or marginalization of disconcerting themes such as imperialism, militarism, and the large-scale killing of noncombatants.

For a nation in the habit of classifying itself as exceptional, these are distressing subjects, despite the fact that each looms large in our past. Yet situating the United States in the emerging Next Order will require coming to terms with them. As with race, a reckoning with these contradictions can no longer be deferred. It's time to come clean.

"Power," John Adams once observed, "always thinks it has a great soul and vast views beyond the comprehension of the weak; and that it is doing God's service when it is violating all His laws."[11] Those words apply to the United States as much as to any other great nation in modern times. Over the course of its national existence, the United States has done important and admirable things. It has also committed grave sins.

First among them is imperialism. Subjecting people deemed inferior to rule by those claiming to be superior is a great evil. Yet the United States has its own rich tradition of imperialism, both formal and informal, dating from the very founding of the Anglo-American colonies.

George Orwell once wrote that people "feel that a thing becomes different if you call it by a different name."[12] Americans have habitually relied on different names to cloak U.S. imperialism: Manifest Destiny, settling the frontier, converting the heathen, protecting American lives and property, and sharing the blessings of democracy. But the presumed beneficiaries of U.S. ministrations, be they Native Americans, Mexicans, Cubans, Filipinos, Vietnamese, or, in more recent days, Iraqis and Afghans, have never been fooled.

Nor should we fool ourselves. In particular, Americans can

no longer afford to overlook the consequences resulting from imperial meddling gone awry. Examples include overthrowing the democratically elected government of Iran in 1953, which permanently poisoned U.S.-Iranian relations; the epic miscalculation of the Bay of Pigs in April 1961, which set in motion the events leading to the Cuban Missile Crisis of the following October; and complicity in the assassination of South Vietnamese president Ngo Dinh Diem in 1963, which destabilized that country and drew the United States ever deeper into a prolonged and ugly quagmire; and, of course, the misguided wars launched in the wake of 9/11 pursuant to a Freedom Agenda that produced dubious benefits while exacting very heavy costs.

Second comes militarism, which Americans are inclined to attribute to armed-to-the-teeth Europeans who rushed headlong into the inferno of the First World War, or to the Germany that emerged from that terrible conflict intent on having another go at it. Yet if militarism manifests itself in romanticizing soldiers, seeing military might as the truest measure of national greatness, and indulging in outsize expectations regarding the efficacy of force, then the United States in our time compares with Prussia during the heyday of Chancellor Otto von Bismarck and Field Marshal Helmuth von Moltke.[13] Numbers tell the story: a Pentagon budget easily surpassing that of any plausible combination of adversaries; some eight hundred military bases scattered in some 140 countries around the globe; and a penchant for armed intervention that finds U.S. forces perpetually at war. Militarism costs a lot; the payoff is negligible.

Third, and most troubling of all, is U.S. involvement in the intentional killing of noncombatants, which is always wrong and can never be justified by "military necessity." The United States once held to this very position. On September 1, 1939,

President Franklin Roosevelt sent an "urgent appeal" to the belligerents in the war that was just beginning in Europe. In it, he asked each government to affirm that it would "in no event, and under no circumstances, undertake the bombardment from the air of civilian populations." Air attacks targeting civilians amounted to nothing less than "inhuman barbarism," Roosevelt wrote.[14]

Needless to say, the recipients of FDR's note ignored his appeal. By 1942, Roosevelt himself effectively disowned it. Targeting civilians became a central component of the American way of war. The ensuing Anglo-American Combined Bomber Offensive killed an estimated 410,000 German civilians.[15] U.S. strategic bombing attacks on Japanese cities killed comparable numbers, including between 80,000 and 100,000 noncombatants during the March 9–10, 1945, firebombing of Tokyo and at least another 225,000 in early August resulting from just two atomic bombs.[16] During the Korean War, beginning in June 1950, a comprehensive campaign aimed at leveling North Korean cities exterminated a million or more noncombatants.[17] And from the mid-1960s to the early 1970s, U.S. air attacks across several Southeast Asian countries killed at least another half million.[18]

The numbers are only estimates. In truth, we can no more tabulate how many civilians were killed by made-in-the-USA fragmentation, incendiary, cluster, or atomic munitions since the 1940s than we can calculate the number of people who died during the Stalinist purges of the 1930s or the Cultural Revolution that Mao Zedong launched in the mid-1960s. All we can say for certain is that the death toll exacted by U.S. bombing was massive and correlated imperfectly at best with intended political outcomes.

Sadly, the U.S. policy of maintaining at the ready a large nuclear arsenal means that even today a further recurrence of "inhuman barbarism" remains a frightening possibility.

The point of offering this interpretation of America's past is not to wallow in our failings or to suggest that we owe the world an apology. Nor am I hinting at a moral equivalence between our transgressions and the horrendous crimes of others.

Yet to know where the nation needs to position itself in the Next Order requires first a clear-eyed account of how it got to where it finds itself today. As Americans consider their future role in the world, they can ill-afford to flinch from a past that includes both much to celebrate and much to regret.

Sadly, no political figure of national stature is likely to subscribe to such a balanced assessment of America's past. Honesty doesn't win elections. Artful hedging in the case of someone like Joe Biden—or crude duplicity in the case of Donald Trump—does. Yet absent honesty, it is hard to see how Americans will arrive at an adequate understanding of their present predicament.

Niebuhr, For Real This Time

Donald Trump's election to the presidency in 2016 symbolized a repudiation of all that Madeleine Albright and her fellow mandarins stood for. Yet Trump's four years as president did not yield anything approximating an alternative. Nor, in all likelihood, will a Biden presidency produce one. Candidate Biden surrounded himself with members of the post–Cold War foreign policy establishment devoted to preserving a global Pax Americana, not to taking a different course.

To understand how a warts-and-all interpretation of America's past could shape U.S. policy going forward, we will have to look elsewhere. In that regard, Reinhold Niebuhr (1892–1971) just might have something to teach us. A unique figure in U.S. history, Niebuhr wielded great influence as a pastor, theologian, teacher, political activist, and public intellectual. From the 1930s to the 1960s, he was arguably the most important figure on the American scene who did not hold high office, command troops in wartime, or preside over some vast industrial, financial, or journalistic domain.

That Arthur Schlesinger dedicated his *Crisis of the Old Order* to his friend Niebuhr was emblematic: If the New Order had a prophet, it was Niebuhr. When he died in 1971, a long, worshipful obituary began on the front page of the *New York Times*. Niebuhr had mentored "scores of men," it read, who comprised "the brain trust of the Democratic Party in the nineteen-fifties and sixties." Among those mentioned were not only Schlesinger, but also Dean Acheson, George Kennan, Paul Nitze, and McGeorge Bundy, all of whom occupied positions of power during or after World War II. Kennan, the ultimate Cold War sage, went so far as to describe Niebuhr as "the father of us all," that *us* referring to the eminences who presided over U.S. policy during the New Order, as, in their judgment, they were meant to do.[19]

In practice, however, Niebuhr was honored more than heeded. He was respected rather than listened to. In retrospect, we can easily see why. Niebuhr taught that power combined with pride induces blindness, leading first to folly and then to tragedy. Members of Washington's postwar policy elite found it inconceivable that this warning should apply to them.

Niebuhr cautioned specifically against the temptation to believe that the United States was called upon to manage history "in accordance with a particular conception of its end."

America's own past, he wrote, was itself "a refutation in parable of the whole effort to bring the vast forces of history under the control of any particular will, informed by a political ideal."[20]

In the eyes of Acheson, Kennan, Nitze, Bundy, and others in their circle, history cried out to be managed. Who else but Americans like themselves could shoulder such an important task? Decades before Madeleine Albright coined the phrase, they had concluded that the United States was, indeed, history's indispensable nation. Here was the rock on which they built their faith. So while Niebuhr might receive a respectful hearing from those who wielded power, they refused to be constrained by his counsel. Certainly, his strenuous opposition to the Vietnam War did not dissuade the administrations of John Kennedy and Lyndon Johnson—both served by men who admired Niebuhr greatly—from embarking upon and continuing that perilous misadventure.[21]

Yet not unlike the poet or composer whose works are suddenly understood after long having been misconstrued, Niebuhr's moment may finally have arrived. Niebuhr agreed with Donald Trump that the United States is anything but innocent. As a Christian, his worldview derived from a belief in Original Sin. All persons are, therefore, fallible and prone to shortsightedness, selfishness, and error. So, too, are all nations. As for God's purposes, they remain unknowable. American Exceptionalism is, therefore, at best illusory and at worst blasphemous. Here was the rock on which Niebuhr built his own quite different faith as a public intellectual.

That said, Niebuhr did not intend for the United States to remain passive in the face of evil. He was neither an isolationist nor a pacifist. Nor was he a utopian. The art of statecraft, in his view, consisted of "finding proximate solutions to insoluble problems." Niebuhr urged policymakers to cultivate "a sense of awe before the vastness of the historical drama in which we are jointly involved" along with "a sense of modesty about the virtue, wisdom, and power available to us for the resolution of its perplexities."[22] In Washington throughout the decades of the New Order, such modesty and awe proved to be in notably short supply. Especially after the Soviet Union imploded and the Cold War ended, with the universal triumph of liberal democracy now taken as a foregone conclusion, the nation's capital was awash in immodesty and self-awe.

How might Niebuhr's emphasis on self-awareness, humility, and prudence—his advocacy of realism combined with moral responsibility—find application in the Next Order that now beckons? The chapters that follow will explore the application of Niebuhrian moral realism to specific challenges awaiting the United States as it leaves the New Order behind.

Niebuhr's conception of moral realism began with a recognition that the primary duty of any government was to provide for the well-being of its citizens. In the case of the United States, that meant keeping Americans safe and preserving their freedoms. This describes what citizens rightly expect from their political leaders, those expectations only heightened by the various policy failures that culminated in the grotesque mishandling of the coronavirus pandemic.

Niebuhrian realism also acknowledged that absolute disregard for the plight of others is neither morally acceptable nor, in an interconnected world, even feasible. The cause of justice, Niebuhr wrote in 1942, is best served "neither by the Utopians who dream dreams of perfect brotherhood nor yet by the cynics who believe that the self-interest of nations cannot be overcome," but by "the realists who understand that nations are selfish" and will remain so, "but that none of us, no matter how selfish we may be, can be only selfish."[23]

The United States possesses neither the wisdom nor the wherewithal to repair a broken world. Yet moral realism demands that nations, including ours, act within their capacity to correct injustice and alleviate suffering. The art of statecraft lies in finding ways to satisfy that requirement, while ensuring that the state's obligation to care for its own citizens remains paramount and also keeping in mind the text of the Hippocratic Oath: "First, do no harm."

As Americans ought to have learned by now, crusades are almost always ill-advised. As a basis for statecraft, deliberation, patience, and self-restraint—leading by example—may offer a far better prospect for success than relying on threats, sanctions, and the use of force.

Of course, a precondition for leading by example is to get one's own house in order. On that score, the Great (if haphazard) Lockdown of 2020, accompanied by another Great Recession, followed that same year by the Great Uprising against racism, with the malevolent presence of Donald Trump presiding over all three, made it abundantly clear that Americans have their work cut out for them.

2

THE ECLIPSE OF THE WEST

Integral to American Exceptionalism is the conviction that the United States belongs to the conglomeration of nations comprising "the West." While Arthur Schlesinger's Old Order prevailed, the ranks of the great powers included several Western nations, with the United States trailing behind Great Britain, France, and (after 1933) Germany in terms of global clout. Since the formation of the New Order, however, America has been primus inter pares. That Captain America should lead the West has become something of a solemn obligation, both symbolizing U.S. global primacy and providing a rationale for the exercise of American power far beyond the boundaries said to define the West. Underlying this arrangement is an unspoken assumption: Who leads the West leads the world.

The arrival of the Next Order renders the very concept of the West obsolete. Except as a repository of sentiment, it serves no purpose. Rather than indulging that sentiment further, the United States would be better served to reposition itself as a nation that stands both apart from and alongside other members of a global community. No longer aspiring to dominion, America should focus on subsuming differences and bridging gaps, an approach likely to be congenial to its own well-being and to the world's.

Throughout the early history of the United States, Americans preferred to think of themselves as located within a self-contained New World. Encompassing the entire Western Hemisphere, that New World existed at some remove from the Old World. As President James Monroe famously put it in 1823, Europe's political system was "essentially different" from that which existed in the Americas, so much so that the United States would regard "any attempt on their part to extend their system to any portion of this hemisphere as dangerous to our peace and safety."[1] Protecting our system meant standing aloof from theirs, a position Monroe's successors endorsed, without, of course, consulting any of this nation's neighbors to the south.

Only in 1917, pursuant to U.S. entry into World War I, did Americans discover that they were politically part of the modern West. The curriculum that came to be called Western Civ originated as a wartime expedient designed "to teach soldiers what it was they would be fighting for in Flanders Fields."[2] Western Civ began, in short, as an exercise in government indoctrination.

This exercise persisted after the armistice and soon gained popularity on university campuses. According to the historian William H. McNeill, Western Civ enrolled Americans, hitherto regarded as raw and unrefined, in "the great cultivated, reasonable, sophisticated world of 'us,' the heirs of a Western tradition dating from Socrates." The onset of World War II and then the Cold War reinforced the importance of situating the

United States within this larger intellectual and cultural community. Western Civ thereby bolstered "the agenda of a unified West led by America fighting for freedom and reason and tolerance," while standing steadfast against tyrannies from the East.

Of course, identifying the West with freedom, reason, and tolerance required a certain sleight of hand—a bit like crediting Christians with actually following the teachings of Jesus. According to a probably apocryphal story, a journalist once asked Mahatma Gandhi, "What do you think of Western civilization?" Gandhi supposedly replied, "I think it would be a good idea."

For those like Gandhi who were not considered bona fide members of the West, the very term was synonymous with empire and white supremacy. After all, leading Western nations, the United States included, were racist to the core. Even after World War II, exemplars of Western values such as Great Britain and France had no intention of surrendering the imperial privileges they had long enjoyed among the Black, brown, and Asian peoples of the world. In its heyday as the enemy of tyranny, in other words, the West retained a sordid underbelly characterized by prejudice, repression, and violence.

In his famous 1946 "Iron Curtain" speech, Winston Churchill declared that the primary purpose of the postwar project was to guarantee "the safety and welfare, the freedom and progress, of all the homes and families of all the men and women in all the lands."[3] It was not the safety, welfare, freedom, and progress of Indians, Egyptians, Iranians, and Kenyans that the former prime minister had in mind. He was referring to Americans, Britons, and citizens of what were then still known as the "white dominions." In other words, Churchill was addressing the "English-speaking peoples" who, along with Europeans classified as sufficiently friendly—"our" (West) Germans, yes, "their"

(East) Germans, no—comprised the postwar West, known then as the "Free World." As for everyone else, well, their fate was their own business.

By the late 1960s, Western Civ was falling out of favor in the classroom. Even so, within Washington and other allied capitals, the idea of a broadly cohesive Free World subscribing to a common set of values and led by the United States survived. As long as international politics centered on the Cold War, a mechanism for distinguishing between *us* and *them* and highlighting the moral superiority of our side retained value that more than compensated for any lack of empirical precision.

That said, with the end of the Cold War, policymakers in Washington embraced the idea of the West with more fervor than ever. This was probably inevitable. The advantages accruing to Captain America were too great to give up merely because the Soviet Union had expired and the People's Republic of China had discovered the wonders of capitalism.

No one played a greater role in imparting to the West a new lease on life than Samuel P. Huntington, the preeminent political scientist of his generation. In the summer of 1993 Professor Huntington published an essay that future scholars are likely to classify among the urtexts signaling the coming demise of American primacy. "The Clash of Civilizations?" stands in relation to the post–Cold War Pax Americana as Case Yellow, the Wehrmacht plan for invading France in 1940, did to Germany's Thousand-Year Reich: It cast a pernicious spell and underwrote the abandonment of reason.

A masterpiece of crispness, elegance, and good timing, Huntington's "Clash" provided the American national security apparatus with a template for thinking about the future that made actual thinking unnecessary. It answered questions that had yet to be asked.

The global future, Huntington wrote, would be defined by interactions among a handful of distinct "civilizations," with competition among them taking the place of outmoded rivalries among princes, nations, or ideologies. In determining the emerging world order, only three such civilizations really mattered, those that Huntington labeled Western, Confucian, and Islamic. Peaceful coexistence among the three would not come easily. Conflict involving at least two if not all three was highly likely. "The next world war, if there is one," Huntington warned, "will be a war between civilizations," in all probability pitting the West against "the Rest."[4]

To offset this ominous prospect, Huntington offered some good news. "Now at an extraordinary peak of power in relation to other civilizations," the West enjoyed enormous competitive advantages.

> Western military power is unrivaled. Apart from Japan, the West faces no economic challenge. It dominates international political and security institutions and with Japan international economic institutions. Global political and security issues are effectively settled by a directorate of the United States, Britain and France, world economic issues by a directorate of the United States, Germany and Japan. . . . Decisions made at the U.N. Security Council or in the International Monetary Fund that reflect the interests of the West are presented to the world as reflecting the desires of the world community. The very phrase "the world community" has become the euphemistic collective

noun (replacing "the Free World") to give global legitimacy to actions reflecting the interests of the United States
and other Western powers.

So things appeared to Harvard's Professor Huntington in
1993. All that remained for the United States, as the West's
unquestioned kingpin, was to exploit these advantages, thereby
keeping "the Rest" in line.

Among scholars specializing in international relations, Huntington's essay touched off fierce controversy.[5] Not in policy circles, however. There, the image of the United States occupying
the center of interlocking directorates that would control the
destiny of the planet meshed nicely with existing perceptions.

This was, after all, a mere four years after the fall of the Berlin
Wall and two years after Operation Desert Storm had subjected
the Iraqi dictator Saddam Hussein to a well-deserved spank-
ing. Together, these two events cemented the impression that
the United States had ascended to the very apex of power, both
within the West and globally. When Bill Clinton, just weeks
after being inaugurated president, told a joint session of Congress that the United States was "the greatest nation on earth"
with "the world's strongest economy, and the world's only military superpower," he was merely telling the assembled worthies
what they already knew to be true.[6]

Paradoxically, however, while American supremacy was self-
evident, it also required continuous affirmation. In political circles, variants of "We're number one!" became a ritualistic chant.

By the time Governor Clinton of Arkansas took that new
job as President Clinton of the Sole Superpower, Niebuhr's
warnings against presuming to manage history sounded fusty
and timid. Opportunity was in the air. The imperative was to

seize the moment. While cautioning that challenges might lie ahead, Huntington had also suggested that civilizational fellow-travelers—he called them "kin-countries"—would willingly enlist to help the United States carry the load in any coming confrontation with "the Rest." Such an arrangement would soften America's image as the global hegemon, in effect styling hegemony as a collaborative enterprise. The West, in other words, would be the vehicle through which the United States would run the world.

Was Huntington's forecast of the global future wrong when he made it? Or did President Clinton and his successors squander the opportunity to build an impregnable Western fortress able to withstand any civilizational challenge? In other words, was the idea of a post–Cold War West misguided or merely mishandled? Today, such questions retain no more than academic interest. What we can say for certain is this: The idea of mobilizing the West as an instrument of U.S. grand strategy barely made it into the next decade. By the time Clinton's successor left office, it had lost all credibility.

The West Unravels

The West came undone for several reasons, but none was more important than this: The end of the Cold War propelled the United States and Europe onto divergent paths. Beginning in the 1990s, Washington succumbed to militarism, embracing an approach to statecraft that relied on the use or threatened use of armed force, with diplomacy an afterthought.[7] The United Kingdom partially (if only momentarily) excepted, European nations did not subscribe to this approach. In Europe, an aversion to militarism, stemming from the experience of the world wars but held in abeyance by the Cold War, now came into full flower. The end of the West, in other words, came about less through some Spenglerian process of decline than through divorce on the grounds of mutual incompatibility.

In a famous essay published in 2002, as the United States was gearing up to invade Iraq, Robert Kagan, historian and neo-conservative polemicist, colorfully but accurately explained why the West was coming apart. "It is time to stop pretending that Europeans and Americans share a common view of the world, or even that they occupy the same world," he wrote.[8]

> On the all-important question of power—the efficacy of power, the morality of power, the desirability of power—American and European perspectives are diverging. Europe is turning away from power. . . . It is entering a posthistorical paradise of peace and relative prosperity, the realization of Kant's "Perpetual Peace." The United States, meanwhile, remains mired in history, exercising power in the anarchic Hobbesian world. . . . That is why on major strategic and international questions today, Americans are from Mars and Europeans are from Venus.

During the first decade after the Cold War, American and European statesmen had collaborated to paper over their differences on "the all-important question of power." During the 1990s, what were styled as Western interventions undertaken to liberate Iraqi-occupied Kuwait, avert mass starvation in Somalia, and end ethnic cleansing in Bosnia and Kosovo were, in practice, U.S. military operations with European window dressing.

For Operation Desert Storm in 1991, the Pentagon deployed

eighteen hundred aircraft; the French air force contributed
forty.[9] The following year, when twenty-five thousand U.S.
troops landed in Somalia, traditional U.S. allies offered to help
feed the starving. When the operation morphed into a nasty
counterinsurgency, however, GIs did the fighting. The rest of
NATO was absent from the battlefield. For Operation Allied
Force, the 1999 air campaign against Serbia, the United States
assembled an armada of over seven hundred aircraft. The Germans kicked in fifteen.[10] Of the thirty-eight thousand sorties
during the campaign, U.S. forces flew more than thirty thousand of them.[11] A more accurate name for Allied Force would
have been American Force with Token Allied Assistance. Taken
as a whole, the contribution of the non-U.S. West to these various undertakings managed to be just slightly above symbolic.

The swan song of the West came in the wake of 9/11. In one
last handsome gesture of Western solidarity, NATO responded
to the attacks on New York and Washington by immediately
declaring that every member of the alliance was thereby under
attack. After decades during which the United States had stood
ready to defend Western Europe, NATO's European members
now affirmed that they were ready and willing to return the favor.

However touching, NATO's offer to shield America from further assaults did not accord with the mood that prevailed in the
White House. The French ambassador to NATO summarized
the U.S. attitude this way: "Well, the Americans said, 'Thank
you. We are very busy now. . . . We'll call you later.'"[12] President George W. Bush had little patience with mere collective
defense; he was keen to retaliate.

For Bush and his key advisers, waging a Global War on
Terrorism meant going on the offensive. To avert subsequent
attacks on the homeland (as it was now called), the United States

needed to root out the underlying causes of terrorism. That necessarily required unleashing the full weight of American military might without delay.

In a memorable address to Congress in January 2002, Bush warned his listeners that "time is not on our side." Mere months before, the Afghanistan War, destined to become the longest in U.S. history, had begun. But in the president's eyes, Afghanistan qualified as a sideshow. He already had his sights set on larger prey. And his eagerness to act was palpable. "I will not wait on events while dangers gather," Bush continued. "I will not stand by, as peril draws closer and closer. The United States of America will not permit the world's most dangerous regimes to threaten us with the world's most destructive weapons. . . . History has called America and our allies to action, and it is both our responsibility and our privilege to fight freedom's fight."[13] The gloves were coming off. As soon became evident, however, the allies Bush had in mind were to serve not as partners but as attendants.

Bush chose not to tell the Congress that he had already made an important decision: Eliminating the root causes of terrorism could not happen without first disposing of a long-standing American nemesis—Iraq's Saddam Hussein. In the White House and the Pentagon, regime change in Baghdad assumed an importance akin to that of World War II's Normandy invasion: This was to be the campaign that would pave the way to final victory.

A year was to elapse before the launch of Operation Iraqi Freedom. In the interim, the invasion that everyone knew was coming dominated conversations not only inside Washington but in allied capitals. The ensuing debate had a surreal aspect: President Bush had already made an irrevocable, if unannounced, decision; nothing that anyone wrote or said, whether for or against, was going to make the slightest difference. Bush was going to do what he felt called upon to do. Even so, the faux Iraq debate that ensued illustrates changes in the way that U.S. policymakers viewed the West: What had been an asset now became a hindrance.

Robert Kagan was prominent among those making the case for ousting Saddam, echoing President Bush's call for action. "The Iraqi threat is enormous," he wrote in a January 2002 essay coauthored with William Kristol. "It gets bigger with every day that passes."

> Ultimately, what we do or do not do in the coming months about Saddam Hussein's regime in Iraq will decisively affect our future security. And it will determine more than that. Whether or not we remove Saddam Hussein from power will shape the contours of the emerging world order, perhaps for decades to come. Either it will be a world order conducive to our liberal democratic principles and our safety, or it will be one where brutal, well-armed tyrants are allowed to hold democracy and international security hostage.

Military victory in Iraq would align the entire Arab world with the West and cement U.S. regional primacy. "A devastating knockout blow against Saddam Hussein, followed by an American-sponsored effort to rebuild Iraq and put it on a path toward democratic governance, would have a seismic impact" on the entire Arab world. "No step," Kagan and Kristol predicted, "would contribute more toward shaping a world order in which our people and our liberal civilization can survive and flourish."

The language that Kagan and Kristol employed nicely summarized views then widely circulating in Washington. Osama bin Laden and nineteen mostly Saudi hijackers had delivered history itself to a pivotal moment. To remain passive was to invite unimaginable ruin. To seize that moment through decisive military action, on the other hand, promised huge benefits for the United States and all of humankind. In such circumstances, preserving the integrity of the West no longer qualified as a priority. Given its overwhelming military superiority, the United States acting alone was fully capable of "shaping a world order" in which liberal civilization would safely thrive.

If America's European allies wanted to pitch in, fine. If not, that was fine, too. While happy to accept whatever modest help a "coalition of the willing" (another phrase briefly au courant) might make available, the United States was prepared to go it alone.

In a Washington where militarists now had the upper hand, going it alone to deliver a "devastating knockout blow" in Iraq seemed eminently plausible. So did all the ancillary benefits that would then presumably follow. In London, Prime Minister Tony Blair had doubts but suppressed them. "I will be with you whatever," he assured President Bush.[14] Blair's submissiveness subsequently earned him the sobriquet of "Bush's poodle."[15]

In Paris and Berlin, however, doubts hardened into opposition. A wide breach opened among leading Western nations. Nor were these differences of opinion concealed from public view.

Addressing the United Nations Security Council in early February 2003, French foreign secretary Dominique de Villepin called for patience, insisting that "the use of force is not justified at this time."

There is an alternative to war: Disarming Iraq via inspections. Moreover, premature recourse to the military option would be fraught with risks. . . . Such intervention could have incalculable consequences for the stability of this scarred and fragile region. It would compound the sense of injustice, increase tension and risk paving the way to other conflicts.[16]

In Germany, a Red-Green coalition government led by Chancellor Gerhard Schroeder and Foreign Minister Joschka Fischer likewise refused to support a preventive war with Iraq. Germany "didn't shy away from offering international solidarity in the fight against international terrorism," Schroeder stated. "But we say this with equal self-confidence: we're not available for adventures, and the time of cheque book diplomacy is over once and for all"—that last a reference to Germany helping to bankroll the Gulf War of 1991 even as it refrained from direct military involvement.[17] This time, if the United States insisted on war, Germany would neither participate nor pay.

Ardent American proponents of invading Iraq did not take kindly to this absence of support from two traditional allies. Hawkish members of the House of Representatives directed that House cafeterias would henceforth list French fries as Freedom Fries and French toast as Freedom Toast. In the eyes of Americans gung ho for war, French reluctance confirmed that nation's reputation as a sanctuary for "cheese-eating surrender monkeys."[18]

Underlying this pettiness was a growing conviction within Washington's pro-war circles that France and Germany no longer mattered. According to Defense Secretary Donald Rumsfeld, they formed part of "old Europe" for which the Bush administration now professed outright contempt.[19] For the United States on the eve of a war certain to result in a "devastating knockout blow," allies had become a convenience rather than a necessity, and Western unity superfluous.

Beyond Repair

The warnings voiced by France and Germany proved prescient. Operation Iraqi Freedom did not produce the results that its architects and cheerleaders expected. Instead, the Iraq War proved to be the costliest U.S. foreign policy blunder since Vietnam. Signing on to this misadventure cost Tony Blair his political career and destroyed his reputation.[20]

In the midst of this ongoing cataclysm, the United States mounted a salvage operation. From the cadaver of the West, it extracted bits and pieces that if artfully arranged might have the appearance of a partnership. The result was the Multi-National Force—Iraq. From 2003 to 2009, this conglomeration of twenty-nine nations performed a wide range of tasks related to security and training assistance. Lest there be questions about who was in charge, MNF-I operated throughout that period under the direction of the senior American officer in theater, always a U.S. Army four-star general.

While not primarily a combat force, MNF-I did sustain losses, which provide a rough measure of its contribution to the cause. The United Kingdom led the pack with 179 fatalities, followed by Italy with 33 and Poland with 23. Only three other MNF-I member states had losses in double digits, each fewer than twenty. Five national contingents lost but a single soldier. Four others lost two. By comparison, U.S. fatalities in the Iraq War numbered 4,486.[21] The heavy lifting, in other words, fell to the Americans.

Substantively more important than MNF-I were the profit-motivated private contractors that descended on strife-torn Iraq like a plague of locusts following the fall of Baghdad. Here was the real coalition of the willing: dozens of firms eager to lend a hand because they saw in Iraq lucrative opportunities. By 2009, to compensate for a shortage of uniformed troops some fifty contractors were employing a workforce of more than thirty thousand employees.[22] This contractor "army" easily outnumbered every contingent in the MNF-I, with the sole exception of the United Kingdom. In effect, quasi-mercenary entities such as Blackwater and Triple Canopy now superseded "the West," with concern for the bottom line taking precedence over adherence to the laws of war or the promotion of democratic values.

In Afghanistan, meanwhile, a similar story unfolded. There NATO, the West's premier legacy institution, did make an appearance, with member states ponying up contingents to form the International Security Assistance Force (ISAF), the Afghanistan version of MNF-I. Dozens of nations contributed to ISAF, creating the impression of a very grand alliance indeed.[23] Reality belied appearance, however.

At the very outset of the Global War on Terrorism, Secretary of Defense Donald Rumsfeld had declared, "The mission determines the coalition, and the coalition must not determine the mission."[24] Rumsfeld's confidence was matched only by his naïveté. As far as ISAF was concerned, domestic politics governed the coalition, with the mission obliged to adjust accordingly.

The spirit pervading ISAF was this: All for one and one for all (but with caveats). Those caveats were restrictions allied governments imposed on what their forces were permitted to do, including the types of operations particular contingents would (or would not) undertake, where they would (or would not) go, and what rules of engagement they would follow. Particularly severe restrictions earned some contingents the derisive title of "ration-consumers" who took up space and used resources but whose contribution to defeating the Taliban was negligible. Commanders also wielded an informal "red card," empowering them to tell ISAF headquarters: We won't do that unless our government says okay and that might take a while.[25]

In any coalition, in any war, there is bound to be friction. Recall Dwight D. Eisenhower as supreme commander in Europe during World War II having to put up with the constant aggravations of the obnoxious British Field Marshal Bernard Law Montgomery.

Yet there is this difference: However much Ike and Monty disliked each other, they got the job done. The same cannot be said of either MNF-I or ISAF. In Iraq, MNF-I spent years trying to create effective Iraqi security forces. Put to the test in 2014 when Islamic State militants surged into northern Iraq, those forces fled virtually without a fight. In Afghanistan, ISAF spent years trying to create an army and national police force able to reduce the Taliban to the level of a nuisance. Almost twenty years later success in achieving that goal is nowhere in sight.

After 9/11, in the eyes of U.S. policymakers eager for war, the West had become an impediment. When George W. Bush disregarded allied objections and invaded Iraq, he put the torch to the idea of transatlantic unity as a foundation of mutual security. Once that war went awry, U.S. efforts to reconstitute some version of the West came up desperately short. Something similar occurred in Afghanistan.

Certainly, where specific interests happen to align, collaboration among various members of the old West continues. The anglophone signals intelligence syndicate known as "Five Eyes," a partnership dating from World War II and involving the United States, the United Kingdom, Canada, Australia, and New Zealand, offers a prime example.[26] Yet this is akin to oil companies joining together to thwart proposed environmental regulations. Transactional cooperation does not imply unity.

Today, if the West that once fought the Nazis and contained Communism can be said to exist, it does so mainly as a figure of speech. To pretend otherwise is pointless.

No West, No East

Consider the West the contemporary equivalent of the Holy Roman Empire that Americans of my generation once encountered in junior high World History courses. Long after events drained it of substance, the carcass of the Holy Roman Empire lingered, even if, in Voltaire's words, it was "neither holy, nor Roman, nor an empire." The same can be said of the West: Politicians and journalists still regularly refer to it, but the fears and aspirations that once held things together have lost their rallying capacity.

As with the Holy Roman Empire by the eighteenth century, so, too, with the West in the twenty-first: It survives primarily as the stuff of legend. At the end of director John Ford's film *The Man Who Shot Liberty Valance*, a cynical newspaper reporter declares, "When the legend becomes fact, print the legend." When presidential candidate Joe Biden promised, if elected, to "organize and host a global Summit for Democracy to renew the spirit and shared purpose of the nations of the Free World," he was following that reporter's advice.[27] While this may be a good way to sell newspapers, it is not a sound principle of statecraft.

The United States finds itself today in an era in which it is no longer helpful to refer to the West or the Free World or even to "our liberal civilization," to employ Kristol and Kagan's phrase. The splintering of what was once the West continues. Intent on pursuing an independent course, the United Kingdom has opted out of the European Union. The possibility of Scotland opting out of the United Kingdom now presents itself.[28] On the continent, Poland and Hungary, emergent autocracies, are following a course that is anything but liberal. Although the EU once dangled the possibility of Turkey joining its ranks and thereby incorporating Turkey into the West, that possibility went up in smoke years ago.

In East Asia, meanwhile, China has emerged as preeminent. The chances of Beijing organizing that quarter of the world into anything approximating a coherent bloc are remote at best. Should China aspire to create its own version of Japan's World War II Greater East Asia Co-Prosperity Sphere, it will meet stout resistance, with India, Japan, South Korea, Vietnam, and Australia among the nations that will resist being drawn into China's orbit.

Then there is China's almost stupefyingly ambitious "Belt and Road Initiative," which aims to improve the infrastructure—ports, rails, roads, airports, power plants, communications networks—in nearly seventy countries throughout the underdeveloped world. (A few European nations have also signed on.) Expected investments will exceed a trillion dollars in total.[29]

To the extent that the BRI succeeds—by no means a sure thing—it will no doubt enhance China's global influence. Will Beijing thereby erect its own version of the Holy Roman Empire?

That prospect seems unlikely. What China makes available is investment assistance and engineering skill, not an exportable way of life. In that regard, the geopolitical implications of the BRI are likely to be no more than incidental.

So what kind of world awaits the United States in the wake of our Apocalypse? First of all, it will remain a world of nation-states, each privileging its own well-being above other considerations. No president in U.S. history rivaled Donald Trump when it came to saying things that were utterly false, if not downright preposterous. Even so, when Trump told the United Nations General Assembly in 2017 that he would "always put America first, just like you, as the leaders of your countries will always, and should always, put your countries first," he was merely stating a truism.[30] The coronavirus pandemic of 2020 confirmed that truism. Governments scrambled to protect their own citizens while coming to the aid of others only when it became convenient to do so.[31]

None of this means that nations will find it impossible to cooperate. But such cooperation is likely to be issue-specific. Collaborative relationships will be fluid rather than fixed, stemming from concerns that are concrete and transnational rather than ideological or (per Huntington) civilizational. And in such a world, the United States will be as likely to find partners in Asia, Africa, or Latin America as among the nations that once comprised the West.

Standing in the way of this more flexible and nimble approach to statecraft is the Great White Elephant of the American diplomatic tradition: the North Atlantic Treaty Organization. When the Soviet Empire and then the Soviet Union slid into history's dustbin, the conditions that had made it essential to create NATO vanished. In 1949, Western Europe had been weak and divided. By the early 1990s, in a phrase favored in Washington, it was "whole and free."[32]

Like some diplomatic equivalent of kudzu, however, the alliance not only survived the disappearance of its founding purpose but managed to spread eastward. As a consequence, so, too, did the obligations imposed on the United States pursuant to the concept of "collective security." Today, Washington finds itself obliged to defend an array of European nation-states that are fully capable of defending themselves.

Conceptually, collective security implies shared burdens and mutual obligations to keep a common threat at bay. As implemented by NATO, the phrase has come to mean something quite different. "Collective" provides a rationale for European allies to off-load onto the United States more than its fair share of the costs required to ensure that Europeans can sleep peacefully in their beds at night. And "security" in this context has an exceedingly narrow definition: It encompasses protection from direct military threats and little more.

Back in the 1950s, when the United States and its allies worried about the Soviet-led Warsaw Pact overrunning Western Europe, this approach to collective security may have made sense. Today, however, when the proximate threats to European security are more varied and not susceptible to military solutions—formations of armored vehicles won't keep undocumented refugees from coming ashore or slow the impact of climate change—it makes no sense whatsoever. For the United States, defending Europe once ranked as Job #1. Today it is a job best left to Europeans. NATO has become an exercise in nostalgia, an excuse for pretending that the past is still present.

There is a larger grand strategic rationale for the United States terminating its membership in NATO. The ultimate goal of U.S. policy is—or ought to be—to foster the creation of a worldwide community of law-abiding nations living in harmony with one another—if not perpetual peace, at least mutual coexistence. Europe today testifies to the feasibility of that goal. The enterprise dating from December 1941 with U.S. entry into the ongoing European war has succeeded. The United States should, therefore, seize the opportunity to proclaim "Mission Accomplished" and move on to more pressing matters.

During most of the twentieth century, international politics centered on conflicts between liberalism and totalitarianism, between white and non-white, between imperialism and national liberation. In the twenty-first century, it will—or at least should—center on reducing inequality, curbing the further spread of militant fanaticism, and averting a total breakdown of the natural world.

Such circumstances will require new approaches to international leadership. Rather than emphasizing threats and coercion, effective leadership must begin with the creation of exemplary communities at home, communities that can serve as models for others to embrace. If the United States aspires to lead the Next Order, it should begin by amending its own failings.

3

NOT SO SPECIAL

Repairing the damage inflicted by the American Apocalypse in 2020 will require the United States to reimagine its role in the world. In that regard, shedding any residual nostalgia for a West that today exists only in the imagination will mark a necessary first step. But belief in a spurious community of Western nations is only one source of illusion from which policymakers will have to free themselves. Repositioning an "indispensable nation" that in recent years has appeared anything but indispensable will also entail reexamining hitherto unquestioned relations with countries with which Americans believe they share a particular affinity, intimacy, and sense of common purpose.

A nation imagining itself to have a special friendship with another country invariably deceives itself and thereby loses sight of its own interests. It also risks exposing itself to manipulation. In his Farewell Address, President George Washington famously warned against "passionate attachments" that foster illusions of common interests, while exposing the United States to "the insidious wiles of foreign influence."[1] The centuries since have validated the wisdom of Washington's counsel.

The apparently special relationship between the United States and China from the first decades of the nineteenth century until the midpoint of the twentieth offers a cautionary illustration, its relevance to the present moment undiminished by the passage of time. From a U.S. perspective, that relationship was a tutorial one. China represented an ancient civilization but one in desperate need of being revitalized and modernized, this at a time when modernity was synonymous with Western, white, Christian, and, above all, American.[2]

During China's "Century of Humiliation," foreign powers had subjected it to various forms of imperial abuse. While itself present in China throughout this period, the United States styled its purposes as different and benevolent. With no professed ambitions to carve out an exclusionary sphere of influence, it pursued an "Open Door" policy advertised as offering equal opportunity in trade and investment to all. Advertised purpose did not equal actual intent. The real purpose of that open door was to give the United States an edge in exploiting China while striking a benign pose. It exemplified the anti-colonial imperialism that was to remain a signature of American statecraft throughout the twentieth century.

Complementing the Open Door was a large-scale program of educational and moral uplift. Thousands of American missionaries, some remaining at their posts for decades, established schools in which they sought to impart the reigning precepts of modernity to the Chinese people. For Americans, therefore, the fabled "China Market" combined both commercial opportunity and moral obligation, a seductive and self-gratifying rationale. The ultimate stakes, however, were less about uplift than strategic advantage.

"What the Chinese lack is not intellectual ability," wrote Arthur Henderson Smith, himself an American missionary, in his influential 1890 treatise *Chinese Characteristics*. "It is not patience, practicality, nor cheerfulness, for in all these qualities they greatly excel. What they do lack is *Character and Conscience*."[3] Christianity imparted by well-intentioned Americans would remedy these defects.

Converting the Chinese involved more than just winning souls. "Those who recognize that moral and spiritual forces ultimately rule the world," Smith observed in a subsequent volume, "will increasingly feel that the West owes it to the ancient East to pay-back a part of its age-long debt by helping to lay deep the foundation of an Oriental Christian civilization." The nation sponsoring the creation of that Oriental Christian civilization would necessarily accrue great influence. Or as Smith put it, "To capture this race for Christ means the early conquest of the whole world."[4] So doing good, from a missionary perspective, also carried with it the prospect of the United States, an emerging world powerhouse, doing well.

Endowing all of this with a semblance of plausibility was the conviction that the Chinese people and the American people shared some sort of mystical bond. Intuitive rather than empirical, this conviction resonated widely within American society. No one did more to promote this belief in an essential unity linking China and the United States than Pearl Buck, author of *The Good Earth* and other best-selling novels. Accepting the Nobel Prize for Literature in 1938, Buck put it this way: "The minds of my own country and of China, my foster country, are alike

in many ways, but above all, alike in our common love of freedom," an exquisitely American sentiment.[5]

American belief in a special relationship with China, rooted
in an ostensibly shared devotion to liberty, reached its apotheosis during World War II when the two nations became allies
against Japan. President Franklin Roosevelt himself affirmed
this special relationship. After conferring with Chinese Nationalist leader Chiang Kai-shek in Cairo in November 1943, FDR
took to the airwaves to praise the Generalissimo, perceived as
the very embodiment of China, as a "man of great vision and
great courage and remarkably keen understanding." Roosevelt
assured his fellow citizens that "we and the Republic of China
are closer together than ever before in deep friendship and in
unity of purpose."[6]

This was propaganda designed for domestic consumption.
And like all propaganda, it consisted of half-truths packaged
with untruths. In fact, both before and during the war, Americans availed themselves of and abused their privileged status
in China. Rather than enhancing mutual understanding, the
wartime expansion of the U.S. military presence in China produced just the opposite—contempt on the part of GIs, anger and
alienation on the part of Chinese who came into contact with
U.S. troops.[7]

Strangely, even today, the myth of a Sino-American special
relationship lingers. As recently as 2018, Vice President Mike
Pence waxed eloquent in recalling when "America and China
reached out to one another in a spirit of openness and friendship."

When our young nation went searching . . . for new
markets for our exports, the Chinese people welcomed

American traders. . . . When China suffered through indignities and exploitation during her so-called "Century of Humiliation," America refused to join in. . . . When American missionaries brought the good news to China's shores, they were moved by the rich culture of an ancient but vibrant people, and not only did they spread faith; they also founded some of China's first and finest universities. . . . When the Second World War arose, we stood together as allies in the fight against imperialism.[8]

Pence's rendering of history is almost comically misleading. It is also illuminating. It neatly recalls the hallucinations to which some U.S. officials, more than a few journalists, and many members of the public succumbed in the wake of World War II when the United States "lost China" to the Communists. That China should refuse further tutelage by the United States and instead chart its own path seemed inexplicable. The resulting sense of being spurned and even betrayed was a product of Made-in-the-USA fantasies. In fact, the special relationship with China was entirely the product of American imaginations. Here was a classic case of *special* leading directly to self-deception.

Rule, Britannia!

Today, comparable fantasies inform relations between the United States and two other nations. In 1962, President John F. Kennedy told Israeli foreign minister Golda Meir, "The United States has a special relationship with Israel in the Middle East, really comparable only to that which it has with Britain over a wide range of world affairs."[9] In conferring on Israel and Great Britain such singular status, Kennedy was merely acknowledging a widely accepted and not terribly controversial assumption.

Some sixty years later, Israel and Great Britain still occupy their own distinctive categories in the matrix of U.S. diplomacy. In both cases, however, that ostensibly special relationship has induced distortions in U.S. policy that ill serve American interests. This was true even before the upheavals of 2020. It remains true today, with a critical reassessment of Anglo-American and Israeli-American relations now long overdue.

The special relationship between the United States and Great Britain dates from World War II when an American president, a British prime minister, and a Soviet dictator forged a partnership that ultimately destroyed the Nazi regime of Adolf Hitler.

Josef Stalin hated Hitler; his war centered on defending the Bolshevik Revolution and expanding the Soviet sphere of influence; Winston Churchill hated Hitler; his war centered on preserving the British Empire and preventing Great Britain from falling out of the uppermost ranks of great powers. Franklin Roosevelt also hated Hitler; his war centered on ending the Great Depression and establishing the United States as the preeminent nation on the planet, while affirming the universality of the American way of life. In other words, the Grand Alliance was a bargain based on considerations of power and ambition rather than shared values. Scratch the surface and so it has always been with Anglo-American relations.

Prior to World War II, those relations were not especially cordial. Twice the United States and Great Britain fought wars against each other. During the American Civil War, the British government flirted with supporting the Confederacy, sparking outrage in Washington. In 1917, the United States did belatedly side with Britain in its war against Germany—albeit as an Associated Power rather than a full-fledged Ally. However, the war's disappointing outcome persuaded many Americans that they had been snookered: In the end, the Great War had nothing to do with making the world safe for democracy and everything to do with satisfying "Perfidious Albion's" imperial ambitions. While less than precise, that conclusion was largely correct.

World War II and then the Cold War prompted most Americans to let bygones be bygones. Helped along by the postwar dissolution of the British Empire, a belief that Britain and the United States subscribed to a common set of values and stood shoulder to shoulder in a common cause took hold.

As long as Great Britain fielded a respectable military establishment—punching above its weight, as the saying went—the special relationship offered the United States some substantive benefits. For example, an impressive contingent of over 90,000 British troops served under overall U.S. command during the Korean War.[10] Beginning in the 1950s, however, successive British governments bent on saving money slashed the force structure of the British Army, Royal Navy, and Royal Air Force and then slashed some more. Today the entire British active military establishment consists of 132,000 personnel, drawn from a total population of 66 million.[11] By comparison, the active duty component of the Israel Defense Forces (IDF) is a third larger, even though Israel has a population of only 8.4 million.[12] Militarily, the United Kingdom no longer punches above its weight. As with other European militaries in the twenty-first century, it barely qualifies as a flyweight, on occasion showing a bit of spunk but barely able to throw a punch at all.

What then accounts for the persistence of the U.S. special relationship with Great Britain? While long-standing intelligence-sharing arrangements no doubt retain some value, more important factors are nostalgia, popular culture, and an inexplicable American fascination with British royals.[13] Each of these expressions of ephemera overlaps with and reinforces the others. Substantively, none of them is worth more than the proverbial bucket of warm spit.

This nostalgia has expressed itself most prominently in quasi-worship of Winston Churchill, dead now for well over a half century. Americans have a seemingly insatiable appetite for Churchilliana. In the last two decades alone, he has been box-office magic, with four major theatrical releases plus one made-for-television production memorializing parts of his life in uniformly heroic terms.[14]

It is at least striking, if not altogether odd, that when singling out role models, recent U.S. presidents have preferred Churchill to his American contemporaries such as Roosevelt or Harry Truman or Dwight D. Eisenhower. For decades now, they have kept a bust of Churchill close at hand in the West Wing of the White House as a sort of talisman or evidence of their own bulldog-like fortitude. In American politics, you can't go wrong wrapping yourself in Old Glory or wrapping your arms around Winston Churchill. On the very day of his inauguration in January 2017, Donald Trump "returned" Churchill to the Oval Office, falsely claiming that his predecessor had snubbed the British prime minister's memory.[15]

The American affinity for products of British pop culture also sustains the special relationship. The enduring popularity of rock groups like the Beatles and the Rolling Stones offers one example. So, too, does the James Bond movie franchise, currently numbering twenty-seven films, with more to come. In the typical Bond adventure, thwarting evildoers finds 007 teaming up with earnest if less glamorous CIA counterparts, the results testifying to the unbreakable Anglo-American partnership.

Then there is *Downton Abbey*, the massively popular public television series that ran for six seasons (plus a motion picture sequel). Had it recounted the saga of a well-to-do German, Argentine, or Indian family with its retinue of servants, it's a safe bet that *Downton Abbey* would not have found an audience in the United States. In fact, it became the most widely watched series in the history of the Public Broadcasting System (perhaps helped along by the fact that the male protagonist married an American heiress).[16] When the show finished its run, an exhibit of costumes, hats, jewelry, tableware, and other gewgaws created for *Downton* toured major American cities, with tickets $30 apiece.[17]

Yet as a demonstration of American Anglophilia, *Downton* is nothing compared to the public's fascination with the British royal family. In minute detail and with some approximation of accuracy, two separate television series have recounted the lives of Queen Victoria and her great-great-granddaughter Elizabeth II. Thirty years after her death, Princess Diana still appears on the cover of American celebrity magazines. And Americans just can't get enough of what Charles and Camilla, William and Kate, and Meghan and Harry are up to and who they are at odds with.

The emperor of Japan and his family don't qualify for this sort of pop star treatment. Nor does the king of Saudi Arabia, the emir of Kuwait, the sultan of Brunei, the queen of Denmark, or the Grand Duke of Luxembourg. The American affinity for the House of Windsor is unique. For citizens of a republic that declared its independence from Great Britain in 1776, it is also more than slightly weird.

In one sense, American fascination with the British royal

family appears innocent enough—just another version of the celebrity worship that has been displacing worship of the divine in twenty-first-century America. Yet combined with World War II–related nostalgia, Churchill-mania, and the tsunami of other British cultural imports, the American fixation with the royal family fosters a sense of transatlantic kinship that is otherwise entirely imaginary.

Once upon a time, Americans might have looked to Britain—or more specifically to England—as the "mother country." Addressing the subjects of George III, the Declaration of Independence spoke of "the ties of our common kindred." But if any such ties existed in 1776, they have long since vanished. For a multicultural America, such thinking inhibits self-understanding. It also situates the United States on the wrong side in a world where whites-only clubs have become obsolete.

Having a loose cannon like Boris Johnson occupying 10 Downing Street with the equally dotty Donald Trump in the White House was to be reminded that the United Kingdom and the United States each have their own distinct set of problems and priorities. At certain points, Anglo-American purposes may overlap, but they do not align. So it was even when Churchill and Roosevelt masqueraded as the best of friends, even as each sought to manipulate the other. So it will always be.

Lord Palmerston, prominent nineteenth-century British statesman, famously declared that nations have neither perpetual friends nor eternal enemies, but only permanent interests. Effective statecraft requires never losing sight of that fact. The disturbances stemming from the Apocalypse of 2020 should spur U.S. policymakers to affirm Palmerston's admonition, especially in regard to bilateral relationships in which sentiment has for too long displaced sober calculation.

Devaluing the Anglo-American special relationship is a pre-condition to revaluing U.S. relations with other nations possessing greater immediate relevance to the security of the United States and the well-being of the American people. To cite only two obvious examples, Canada and Mexico each should take precedence over the United Kingdom in any reasoned evaluation of U.S. foreign policy priorities. Our immediate neighbors to the north and south matter infinitely more than a cluster of islands situated off the coast of Europe. The unhappy events of 2020 should prompt Americans to acknowledge that fact.

Plenty of Daylight

It has become the custom among American politicians running for high office to insist that there is "no daylight" between Israel and the United States.[18] Former Israeli ambassador to the United States Michael Oren has added a second principle said to guide U.S.-Israeli relations: "no surprises."[19] In fact, since the founding of the State of Israel in 1948, there has been plenty of daylight between the two nations and no shortage of surprises.

In the autumn of 1956, for example, Israel colluded with Great Britain and France to invade Egypt in an attempt to overthrow its president, Gamal Abdel Nasser. To say that the episode, occurring just days before a presidential election in the United States, caught President Dwight D. Eisenhower unawares is putting it mildly: He was furious. Israel also went to great lengths to conceal its nuclear weapons program from the United States. Presidents inquired; Israeli leaders dissembled.[20] While it is true that the June 1967 Israeli preemptive attack on Egypt did not catch the United States by surprise, the subsequent Israeli air and naval assault on the USS *Liberty*—34

Americans dead, 171 wounded—did. Although the Israeli government described the attack as a tragic accident, the incident has remained controversial, not least among surviving crewmembers.[21]

Then in 1981, Israeli pilots flying U.S.-manufactured fighter-bombers attacked and destroyed an Iraqi nuclear reactor under construction near Baghdad. Again, Israel ignored the no-surprises rule, acting without providing Washington with advance warning. In response, the United States voted in favor of a United Nations Security Council resolution condemning the Israeli action.[22] The following year, the government of Israeli prime minister Menachem Begin blatantly deceived the Reagan administration as to its purposes in invading Lebanon, claiming that Israel intended only to clear Palestinian fighters from a zone in southern Lebanon when in fact the aim was to install a new pro-Israel order in Beirut. Soon thereafter, the Jonathan Pollard case exposed Israel's willingness to recruit American citizens—this one happened to be Jewish—to spy on behalf of Israel. To believe that Pollard, an American traitor viewed by many Israelis as a national hero, was a one-off would require remarkable naïveté.[23] And not least of all, Israeli governments have consistently blown off U.S. opposition to the establishment of Israeli settlements throughout the West Bank. This de facto policy of colonization hugely complicates prospects of the "two-state solution," which successive U.S. administrations (until the Trump presidency) consistently professed to support.

Where security is concerned, in other words, Israeli governments do not abide by principles such as "no daylight" and "no surprises." From an Israeli perspective, the principles employed to manage relations with the United States are "first things first" and "damage control over inaction." *First things first* means that

Israeli governments privilege basic security over all other considerations without exception. *Damage control over inaction* means
that the first principle applies even if that entails defying the
United States.

On one occasion, Israel did depart from those principles.
This occurred in 1991, when the government of Prime Minister Yitzhak Shamir assented to a U.S. request to refrain from
counterattacking when Iraqi SCUD missiles rained down on Tel
Aviv and Haifa, instead allowing U.S. Army Patriot missiles to
deploy to Israel to provide a protective shield. But this became
the exception that proved the rule: The Patriots were ineffective
and Israel thereafter embarked upon a crash program, funded by
the United States, to field its own antimissile defenses.[24] Never
again would it remain passive when facing a threat.

There is much to admire in the single-mindedness with which
Israeli leaders guard the security of the Jewish state. While they
may at times miscalculate, the reckless incursion into Lebanon
offering one example, they never lose sight of what really matters: ensuring the safety and well-being of Israel. Moreover,
while the government of Israel does not hesitate to use force—
the Israel Defense Forces are almost continually engaged in
"mowing the grass"—it expends the lives of Israeli soldiers spar-
ingly.[25] Israel does not charge its armed forces with exporting
Zionism or spreading Jewish values. In contrast to their American counterparts, Israeli policymakers don't send their soldiers
to die in pursuit of ideological fantasies.

Israeli willingness to indulge U.S. policy preferences is directly
proportional to the extent to which those preferences comport
with Israel's own needs. Over time, this unwavering clarity of
purpose, seldom matched in Washington, has imparted to the
Israeli-American special relationship a distinct tilt in Israel's favor.

Back in 1962, when Golda Meir called on President Kennedy, she did so as a supplicant, a senior official of a small state, founded slightly more than a decade earlier, seeking assistance from the world's most powerful nation. Hoping to avert a Middle Eastern arms race, Kennedy's predecessor had refused to sell Israel heavy weapons. With Kennedy in the Oval Office, the Israeli government hoped to reverse that policy, opening the spigot to arms from the United States. The effort succeeded, the Kennedy administration agreeing to sell the State of Israel Hawk antiaircraft missiles for a purchase price of $25 million.[26]

The significance of this decision, prompted in no small measure by Kennedy's desire to shore up his support among Jewish American voters, went far beyond bolstering Israeli defenses against air attack.[27] Arms transfers from the United States henceforth became a concrete, measurable expression of the special relationship between the two countries. The rationale devised to justify these transfers was to ensure that the IDF maintained a *qualitative edge.* But much like, say, *affirmative action* or *politically correct*, that phrase was a euphemism. Properly interpreted, *qualitative edge* signified a U.S. commitment to ensuring unambiguous Israeli military superiority over any and all potential adversaries.

Successive administrations in Washington along with members of both parties in Congress agree that it is incumbent upon the American taxpayer to sustain Israeli military superiority in perpetuity. This obligation finds concrete expression in a subsidy that today stands at $3.8 billion annually, along with billions more in loan guarantees. Through 2019, the United States has provided Israel with $142 billion in non-inflation-adjusted dollars, with another $33 billion promised through 2028.[28] While Washington formerly provided substantial economic support to Israel, today that aid almost exclusively takes the form of "security assistance," another euphemism that, properly translated, means "advanced weaponry."[29]

. No longer a fragile young nation or an underdeveloped one—Israeli per capita GDP now equals that of the United Kingdom—the government of Israel deals with the government of the United States not as a supplicant but (to repurpose a phrase from American popular culture) as a "friend with benefits." No other nation enjoys comparable access to the U.S. Treasury. No other nation enjoys greater sway in American domestic politics.

Today the U.S.-Israeli relationship qualifies as *special* in the sense that the executive and legislative branches of the United States government are uniquely deferential to the Jewish state. To understand what this means in practice, contrast JFK's *sale* of Hawks in 1962, paid for by a U.S. loan repayable over ten years at 3 percent interest, with U.S. funding of Israeli antimissile defenses via *grants* that as of 2018 exceeded $6 billion.[30] While a Pentagon plan to *purchase* Iron Dome antimissile batteries from the Israeli arms manufacturer Rafael broke down due to technical complications, the willingness of U.S. officials to pay for Israeli military hardware created with U.S. taxpayer dollars speaks volumes about which party enjoys the upper hand in the U.S.-Israeli relationship.[31]

Were there any doubts on that score, President Donald Trump resolved them when he moved the U.S. embassy from Tel Aviv to Jerusalem in 2018 and subsequently released a "peace plan" that once and for all pulled the plug on the two-state solution.[32] Both actions delighted the Israeli government. In doing so, of course, Trump abandoned even the pretense of Washington playing the role of honest broker in the Israeli-Palestinian conflict.

Whatever Trump's motives, his actions did yield one useful result. While moving the U.S. embassy and effectively endorsing decades-long Israeli efforts to forestall the creation of a viable Palestinian state might accord with Israeli interests, there is no way to make a case that his decisions served the interests of the United States. In other words, by 2020, the special relationship was clearly working for Israel, but it wasn't particularly working for the United States.

No doubt inadvertently, Trump thereby made it permissible to pose questions about the U.S.-Israeli relationship previously regarded as off-limits. Just as Great Britain is no longer the nation that valiantly stood alone against Hitler in 1940, so, too, Israel is no longer the frail and isolated newborn state of 1948. Rather than weak and vulnerable, Israel today is affluent and powerful, perfectly capable of defending itself against its remaining enemies, their ranks rapidly diminishing. As Martin Indyk, peace process veteran and twice U.S. ambassador to Israel, has written, Israel today is fully able to "defend itself by itself." Furthermore, he notes, "it is today's nuclear-armed Israel that has the means to crush Iran, not the other way around."[33] No one has ever accused Indyk of being insufficiently attuned to Israel's well-being.

So what's the harm? For the United States to persist in categorizing its relationships with Britain and Israel as special is akin to clinging to imperial pretensions even after the costs of maintaining the empire exceed the benefits. Sentiment and nostalgia inhibit realistic analysis. By extension, they promote miscalculation not only among the partners in the relationship but among others as well.

For example, expectations of the Anglo-American special relationship leading to an advantageous trade deal with the

United States arguably encouraged the British government to expect a relatively painless departure from the European Union. In fact, the United States is unlikely to come to Britain's rescue as it did in 1941 with Lend-Lease. Specialness goes only so far.

Similarly, the Israeli-American special relationship has created the impression in some quarters that Iran represents a common threat to both nations. It does not. Yet that impression has had the effect of locking the United States into a confrontational posture toward the Islamic Republic. The effect has been to inhibit Washington's diplomatic flexibility in the Persian Gulf, obliging it to take sides in disputes that are extraneous to core American interests.

The argument here is not for cutting ties with the United Kingdom or Israel but for normalizing them. Relations with these two nations ought to resemble relations between the United States and various other countries with which the United States maintains a cordial connection: plenty of trade, investment, tourism, and good wishes, but with no particular expectations, no obligations, and above all no further illusions.

4

STRANGE DEFEATS,
AMERICAN-STYLE

On the eve of the Apocalypse of 2020, the U.S. Army weighed in with its own authoritative interpretation of the Iraq War.[1] Appearing in two volumes, totaling more than fourteen hundred pages of text, maps, illustrations, and scholarly apparatus, *The U.S. Army in the Iraq War* relegated that conflict to the past, ignoring the fact that several thousand GIs remain present in what the Pentagon still classified as a war zone.

If arguably a tad premature, the army's history pulls no punches. It candidly inventories various "systemic failures" that marred the war's conduct. "Highly intelligent, highly experienced leaders" made decisions that "seemed reasonable at the time they were made" but nonetheless resulted in "strategic defeat."[2] The verdict is unvarnished, striking, and severe, offered without excuse or apology.

Few Americans took note of these severe judgments. Tell-all books about Donald Trump and his bizarre presidency garnered press attention and sold. Weighty tomes thick with endnotes about controversial armed conflicts that most Americans were inclined to forget did not. The army's take on its experience in Iraq attracted few reviews and, one suspects, fewer readers.[3] Within national security circles, its impact was so slight as to be undetectable.

Doubtless, a similar fate awaits the army's official account of the Afghanistan War, when it appears at some future date— assuming, that is, that the United States does eventually manage to extricate itself from its longest war ever.

As episodes in American history, the post-9/11 conflicts in Afghanistan and Iraq seem destined to fade into memory as the equivalent of the conjoined twins that the nineteenth-century impresario P. T. Barnum exhibited as curiosities: two separate entities fused together, obscuring the distinctive identity of each. In fact, however, the tissues connecting the Afghanistan War and the Iraq War are no more substantial than those that connected America's wars against Nazi Germany and Imperial Japan. Simultaneity does not connote a substantive relationship.

Ironies that complicate efforts to understand what the Afghanistan and Iraq Wars actually signify begin here. When launched in 2001 and 2003, respectively, these two largest post-9/11 U.S. military campaigns were marketed as components of an ambitious Global War on Terrorism. That formulation was, in fact, little more than a cover story. The GWOT, as it was dubbed, was an artifice designed to disguise a neo-imperial enterprise, its unacknowledged purpose to pacify and transform a large swath of the Islamic world, relying on American military power to achieve that end.

However large the gap between name and actual purpose, the undertaking did not unfold as its architects in Washington expected. Soon enough, the wars in Afghanistan and Iraq veered off on divergent trajectories, each marked by its own grand pronouncements, false dawns, and deep disappointments. For years, Iraq claimed the preponderance of Washington's attention and resources, Afghanistan figuring as an afterthought. Neither went well. In the process, the Global War on Terrorism unceremoniously devolved into its component parts. The phrase itself faded from common usage.

Even so, resurrecting the pretense that those two unrelated wars once comprised a single unified undertaking sheds light on another crucial illusion that the Apocalypse of 2020 should encourage Americans to acknowledge and then shed: the illusion of U.S. military supremacy.

Twice in the first decade of the twenty-first century, the world's preeminent military establishment—the best in all of history by some estimates—embarked upon a war against a markedly inferior adversary. Both campaigns began with high expectations of victory. What actually materialized, however, was indistinguishable from defeat.

Shock and Awe

Considered strictly from a military operational perspective, why did inaugurating a Global War on Terrorism ever seem like a good idea? What invested that proposition with plausibility?

The answer is to be found in a profound misreading of recent military history. In the wake of Operation Desert Storm in 1991—a brief campaign against a weak, ineptly led enemy interpreted as a triumph of world historical significance—the notion took hold in military, political, and media circles that the United States had achieved or was on the brink of achieving absolute mastery over war itself.

Tracing the origins of a truly bum idea can pose challenges, not least of all because its proponents devote themselves to covering their tracks. A century after the Eighteenth Amendment outlawed "the manufacture, sale, or transportation of intoxicating liquors" in the United States, it's difficult to find any figure in American public life willing to make the case that Prohibition deserves a second chance. Or consider the infamous "war on drugs" dating from the 1970s: Having filled prisons with mostly brown and Black inmates while leaving intact a robust American appetite for getting high on illegal substances, today it finds few defenders. And while the Laffer curve may still retain some appeal among eccentrics, serious people have long since rejected the crackpot theory that slashing tax rates offers a sure-fire recipe for increasing total tax revenues.

Something similar applies to the ambitious military reform project undertaken by the Pentagon following the Cold War. To say that it did not pan out as expected is an understatement.

The stated aim of that undertaking, styled as the Pentagon's Joint Vision, was to achieve nothing short of "Full Spectrum Dominance," imparting to the armed forces qualities that would make them "persuasive in peace, decisive in war, [and] preeminent in any form of conflict."[4] Published in 1996 and updated in 2010, the Joint Vision described in colorful detail the expected character of future armed conflict and the institutional changes that would enable U.S. forces "to defeat any adversary and control any situation across the full range of military operations."

Packed with fluff and clogged with jargon, the Joint Vision necessarily required decoding. While signaling the need for fundamental change, it simultaneously offered plentiful reassurances to those with turf to protect: The approaching future would respect the legacies of the past. Change need not inflict pain. Don't worry: Your rice bowl is safe.

An equivalent Joint Vision published in 1940 would surely have included favorable mention of the horse cavalry units still on the rolls of the U.S. Army while foreseeing a long life for battleships such as those destined to end the following year resting in the mud on the bottom of Pearl Harbor. That said, we can summarize the Joint Vision's essence in a single sentence: *Advanced information technology will determine the outcome of future wars of all types, in all environments, anywhere in the solar system.*

When the United States initiated its post-9/11 wars in Afghanistan and Iraq, actual implementation of the Joint Vision was still a work in progress. U.S. forces entering those two countries did not yet possess the full panoply of capabilities supposedly required to guarantee Full Spectrum Dominance. Yet utopian visions propagated from on high invariably shape expectations in the here and now.

Senior civilian officials like Defense Secretary Donald Rumsfeld had already bought into the idea that, as one skeptic put it, "a Slim-Fast military, equipped with the latest technological gizmos, could defeat a foe overnight."[5] Tommy Franks, the four-star general who commanded the Afghanistan and Iraq Wars through their initial stages, was another true believer. When Franks briefed reporters as Operation Iraqi Freedom began to unfold in March 2003, he offered a fair imitation of a snake oil salesman hawking his wares. The campaign just beginning, he promised, would be "unlike any other in history, a campaign characterized by shock, by surprise, by flexibility, by the employment of precise munitions on a scale never before seen, and by the application of overwhelming force." The fighting would conclude in short order, with decisive victory the assured outcome. Franks all but promised a money-back guarantee to any dissatisfied customer.

Reporters quickly embraced a tagline to describe this dazzling new American way of war: They called it "shock and awe."[6]

As it turned out, however, shock and awe was to war what Donald Trump's promotion of hydroxychloroquine as a cure for coronavirus was to the pandemic of 2020: a con job that wreaked havoc on the lives of untold innocents. Rather than validating the Joint Vision's expectations of war transformed by information technology, the indecisive conflicts that tied down U.S. troops in Afghanistan and Iraq told a different story. U.S. forces did indeed enjoy a clear-cut technological edge. But technology did not produce victory. Put to the test, the Pentagon's Joint Vision flopped.

War in the Ether, War in the Dirt

Why did this blueprint for achieving global military supremacy come up short? It did so, at least in part, because the Joint Vision discounted war's political dimension. After the Cold War, when the American technological edge over any potential adversary appeared insurmountable, the Pentagon framed war as primarily a technological enterprise. In that sense, U.S. military planners committed a categorical error: They assumed an enemy that would obligingly play to America's strong suit.

U.S. military operations after 9/11 took place in two distinct arenas. But they were not Central Asia and the Persian Gulf. They were in the air and on the ground. In the air, U.S. forces managed to implement some approximation of the Joint Vision, achieving results that were simultaneously impressive and irrelevant. War on the ground told a different story: There

American soldiers and Marines fought gallantly enough but never came close to achieving victory. It was the complexity of the politics that confounded them.

U.S. air operations since the beginning of the Global War on Terrorism in 2001 testify to the impressive skill and professionalism of American combat aviators. While comprehensive statistics are difficult to come by, air force, navy, and Marine Corps pilots have flown literally millions of sorties since 9/11 while attacking targets with commendable accuracy.[7] Under the guise of conducting "precision" bombing campaigns, prior generations of aviators had literally obliterated whole cities. While deadly errors still marred GWOT air operations, munitions now hit the intended target most of the time, with collateral damage the exception rather than the rule.[8] Except at very low altitudes, U.S. control of the skies above the battlefield in Afghanistan and Iraq was essentially uncontested.

Freedom of action translated directly into an extraordinary level of effort. In support of combat operations in Afghanistan just from 2007 to 2019, for example, American aircrews completed over 215,000 strike sorties, a figure that does not include intelligence, surveillance, reconnaissance, or logistical missions. Between 2008 and 2011, support for Operation Iraqi Freedom included more than 38,000 close air support missions. From 2014 to 2019, Operation New Dawn (successor to Iraqi Freedom) brought another 92,000 strike sorties.[9] Remarkably, given this level of activity, not since the spring of 2003 has the United States lost a fixed-wing military aircraft to enemy action.[10]

As a determinant of outcomes, however, these impressive numbers were the equivalent of the popular vote in U.S. presidential elections: noteworthy, but ultimately not germane.

In framing the new American way of war, the Pentagon's Joint Vision had coined a lexicon of novel terms such as *dominant battlespace awareness*, *asymmetric leverage*, *full spectrum protection*, and *total asset and intransit* [sic] *visibility*. But these arcane phrases never quite completed the jump from PowerPoint aspiration into actual practice.

Ground combat in Afghanistan and Iraq yielded an altogether different lexicon that reeducated Americans regarding the enduring reality of war. Operative terms included IED, TBI, and PTSD. An enemy skilled in deploying *improvised explosive devices* killed or maimed unsuspecting GIs. One result was a spike in *traumatic brain injuries*, which numbered among the factors contributing to an epidemic of *post-traumatic stress disorder*. The Pentagon's Joint Vision had neither anticipated nor prepared for any of these, along with a host of other surprises encountered in Afghanistan and Iraq.

Above the battlefield, air force, navy, and Marine Corps high-performance aircraft and drones operated with virtual impunity. On the ground, despite possessing superior arms and equipment, GIs enjoyed few advantages. Rather than keeping to the tidy pattern envisioned in the Joint Vision, combat in Afghanistan and Iraq did not differ materially from the chaos and confusion that earlier generations of U.S. troops had encountered when pursuing rebellious Filipino nationalists at the turn of the twentieth century or fighting Vietnamese guerrillas in the 1960s. At a certain level, all dirty wars are alike.

Taking the lives of more than six thousand American soldiers while leaving tens of thousands of their comrades with physical or psychological wounds, many of them grievous, the fighting on the ground in Afghanistan and Iraq demolished the Joint

Vision's utopian pretensions. While of only passing interest to most Americans, U.S. interventions after 9/11 also left hundreds of thousands of others dead, while displacing millions.[11] Peace, democracy, and respect for human rights did not flourish as a result.

Commanders who inherited these wars long after visions of quick and easy victory had vanished learned to lower expectations on what they were likely to achieve. Gone was the bombast of General Tommy Franks guaranteeing a big win. That "there is no military solution" to the problems they were charged with solving emerged as a favored explanation.[12] Yet this admission was comparable to Facebook CEO Mark Zuckerberg opining that social media might not, in the end, be such a good idea. After all, ever since the 1990s, a firm conviction that military might *did* offer a solution to whatever threatened the international order over which the United States presided as sole superpower had formed the central premise of U.S. national security policy.

Military power held the key to perpetuating American global primacy: In post–Cold War Washington, this had become tantamount to dogma, nowhere more so than among the generals and admirals who signed off on the Pentagon's Joint Vision. By extension, ousting distant regimes that U.S. policymakers judged unacceptable and installing something better—or at least more agreeable to American sensibilities—would advance this overarching political purpose. Asserting this unique prerogative would therefore testify to American preeminence.

The actual experience of the wars in Afghanistan and Iraq shredded such expectations.

Moving On

The army's official history of the Iraq War cites a long list of errors and misjudgments contributing to strategic failure. Especially telling is a candid admission that the United States lacked sufficient troops on the ground to pacify Iraq, much less to install a new political order. A "de facto cap on U.S. troop strength in Iraq" resulted in "an absolute shortage of ground forces." A future official history of the Afghanistan War will almost surely render a similar verdict. The "historical American predilection to assume technology or qualitative warfighting superiority can be a substitute for troop numbers"—a predilection at the very heart of the Joint Vision—had had fateful consequences.[13] So at least the army's own historians contended.

This problem of too much war and too few soldiers is not a curse delivered from on high. It stems directly from the nation's preferred military system, which finds substantive expression in the so-called All-Volunteer Force (AVF). A wealthy nation with a total population now approaching 330 million, the United States could, if it wished to do so, put a considerably larger contingent of troops on the ground than it did in Afghanistan and Iraq. That it did not do so is an expression of political choice.

(Whether more "boots on the ground" would have produced a more favorable outcome, as the army's history implies, is, of course, a large question. The presence of foreign occupying forces in Afghanistan and Iraq prompted violent resistance. Increasing the number of occupiers might well have simply added fuel to the fire.)

The United States chooses to remain the planet's preeminent military power, indeed, insists on the imperative of doing so. Pursuant to that goal, it chooses to spend enormous sums of money, far greater than any plausible combination of adversaries. Yet it also chooses to relieve citizens of any obligation to participate in implementing national security policy, instead tasking a relatively small cadre of professionals with that responsibility. Choice is the common theme.

Created near the end of the Vietnam War, the All-Volunteer Force has since entrenched itself as a permanent feature of American life. Like Social Security and Medicare, it belongs to the category of arrangements that citizens and elected officials alike tacitly treat as sacrosanct. Yet as the wars in Afghanistan and Iraq demonstrated, the All-Volunteer Force is out of sync with U.S. global ambitions. Even so, as if enshrined in the Constitution, the post-Vietnam military system remains fixed in place.

As a consequence, the problem of too much war and too few soldiers eludes serious scrutiny. Expectations of technology bridging that gap provide an excuse to avoid asking the most fundamental of questions: Does the United States possess the military wherewithal to oblige adversaries to endorse its claim of being history's indispensable nation? And if the answer is no, as the post-9/11 wars in Afghanistan and Iraq suggest, wouldn't it make sense for Washington to temper its ambitions accordingly?

Within a national security apparatus committed to a grand strategy of perpetual global primacy, the question itself is anathema. The Pentagon finds it much more congenial to assume that the next wars will go better than the last ones.

So it was that in the midst of 2020, with the public distracted by a host of pressing concerns, service leaders took it upon themselves to formulate new "visions" aimed at putting the unpleasantries of Afghanistan and Iraq in the rearview mirror. Upon close examination, those new visions bore more than passing resemblance to the thinking that had inspired the Joint Vision in the first place. In essence, the hunt for military supremacy was back on.

Significantly, the resumption of this hunt left no room—none at all—for mulling over recent failures and disappointments. In effect, military leaders chose to repackage and relabel the Joint Vision that had been found so badly wanting in the aftermath of 9/11. Opting to ignore the wars that had preoccupied U.S. forces over the previous two decades, they fashioned theories of wars that they were counting on to prove more agreeable.

So in March 2020, the commandant of the Marine Corps published "Force Design 2030," his template for reform. Premised on a "shift in our primary focus to great power competition and a renewed focus on the Indo-Pacific region," the document contained not a single reference to the Marine experience in Afghanistan or Iraq. Yet the spirit of the Joint Vision's technological utopianism lived on, the Marine Corps committing itself to "develop multi-axis, multi-domain precision fires organic at all echelons, enabled by a federated system of networks"—reviving the post–Cold War penchant for substituting mumbo jumbo for grounded analysis.[14]

In October, the navy drew back the curtain on "Battle Force 2045," a blueprint for increasing the overall size of the fleet to some five hundred ships. The result, then–Defense Secretary Mark Esper promised, would be a "more lethal, survivable, adaptable, sustainable, modern and larger force than we have seen in many years."[15] To emphasize the historical bona fides of Battle Force 2045, Secretary Esper referenced the nineteenth-century naval theorist Alfred Thayer Mahan. But again, the wartime experiences of the previous two decades went unmentioned.

As for the army, it unveiled its vision for the "Army of 2028," which would be ready to "deploy, fight, and win decisively against any adversary, anytime and anywhere." A visitor to the web pages describing the various bits and pieces of this vision will search in vain for any reference to the wars in Afghanistan and Iraq, which absorbed that service's energy and attention for years without producing anything remotely resembling decisive victory.[16]

The officer-historians who labored over the *U.S. Army in the Iraq War* might as well have sent their findings directly to some Pentagon archive of forgotten books. Present-day military leaders have neither any desire nor any intention to learn from the painful experiences of the post-9/11 wars. They have already moved on, busily cultivating an imaginary future more to their liking. During the Apocalypse of 2020, there would be no looking back and, hence, no accountability. Beset with myriad troubles, the American people were in no mood to object. In effect, they tacitly concurred with the Pentagon's preference to move on as if nothing untoward had occurred.

To realize the dangers here, it should hardly be necessary to cite George Santayana's famous dictum about how a past forgotten is a past that recurs. If the dispiriting events of 2020 are to produce anything of value, they ought to prompt Americans to delve more deeply and seriously into their own recent history, both military and otherwise. We have much to learn, and the successive political and strategic defeats that U.S. forces have suffered in the present century offer a place to start.

5

NATURE BITES BACK

On May 11, 1945, two kamikazes slammed into the aircraft carrier USS *Bunker Hill* (CV-17). As the flagship of Task Force 58, the ship was supporting U.S. troops then fighting on the Japanese island of Okinawa. The kamikaze attack proved devastatingly effective, triggering raging fires and setting off numerous secondary explosions. Casualties aboard the carrier were appalling: 393 killed, 264 wounded, and 43 missing.[1] Heroic action by surviving crew members kept the ship afloat. The *Bunker Hill* limped back to Pearl Harbor and then on to the Puget Sound Naval Shipyard for repairs.

Never again would an adversary succeed in rendering a U.S. Navy fleet carrier hors de combat. Never, that is, until the spring of 2020 when COVID-19 knocked the USS *Theodore Roosevelt* (CVN-71) out of action.

The *Roosevelt* is the navy's fourth Nimitz-class nuclear carrier, commissioned in 1986 during the closing phase of the Cold War. Only after the Cold War ended did the "Big Stick" live up to its nickname as it participated in virtually every combat or quasi-combat campaign across thirty years of almost continuous U.S. military activism. During Operations Desert Shield, Desert Storm, Provide Comfort, Deny Flight, Deliberate Force, Allied Force, Southern Watch, Enduring Freedom, Iraqi Freedom, and Inherent Resolve, aircraft operating from the *Roosevelt* conducted tens of thousands of sorties.[2] Throughout this period, no enemy force posed even the approximation of a threat to the ship and its crew. An imposing symbol of U.S. military might, the "Big Stick" seemed invincible.

That turned out not to be so, however. In April 2020, COVID-19 forced the *Theodore Roosevelt* to seek refuge in Guam, where well over a thousand crew members tested positive for the virus and were quarantined. Unlike the kamikazes that in 1945 smashed into the *Bunker Hill*, the virus that sidelined the *Theodore Roosevelt* inflicted no physical damage. Yet the operational effect was the same: A valued asset was rendered unavailable.

The *TR*'s saga captured national attention when the acting navy secretary fired the ship's skipper for having failed to "act professionally." Captain Brett Crozier's offense was to sound the alarm about the danger that COVID-19 posed to members of his crew. With some already infected, Crozier feared—as it turned out, correctly—that many others were at risk.[3]

"We are not at war," he wrote in an emotional letter to his superiors. "Sailors do not need to die. If we do not act now, we are failing to properly take care of our most trusted asset—our Sailors." Inevitably, the letter, which was unclassified, found its way into the media. The leak cost Crozier his job. As he disembarked for the last time, his crew gave him a rousing send-off of the type usually reserved for Super Bowl–winning

quarterbacks.[4] This, too, became national news. The acting
navy secretary promptly flew to Guam, where in an obscenity-
laced presentation he chewed out the crew for supporting their
captain—more national news—and was himself summarily
forced to resign. In the meantime, the now-jobless Captain
Crozier contracted the virus and was himself quarantined on
Guam.[5]

The human-interest angle made the story media catnip.
Yet the ensuing hoopla deflected attention from larger questions
that the plight of the *Theodore Roosevelt* ought to have raised.

"We are not at war," Captain Crozier told his superiors.
While nominally true, that statement was also misleading. In
fact, from the time that Crozier graduated from the U.S. Naval
Academy in 1992, the United States has been at war or gearing
up for war or enforcing no-fly zones or launching humanitarian
interventions that amounted to war-by-another-name.

For the men who had served aboard the *Bunker Hill*, war was
about winning; when it ended, they would go home. For the men
and women assigned to the *Theodore Roosevelt*, winning does not
describe their collective purpose. They are in the business of
national security, an enterprise that by definition is never-ending.
With the rest of the fleet and the other armed services, they
engage in an ongoing cycle of intense activity ostensibly meant
to keep Americans safe and enable them to enjoy freedom.

In the spring of 2020, it became apparent that something
had gone badly awry. Despite the best efforts of the *Roosevelt* and
the rest of the military establishment, Americans felt anything
but safe. They were dying by the tens of thousands. Millions
were losing their jobs. Tens of millions were confined to their
homes. And the "Big Stick," having been knocked out of the
ring, wasn't proving to be of much help. Something was clearly

amiss, even if the United States military appeared oblivious to what that something might be.

The situation was not, in fact, without historical precedent. Some seventy years earlier, in the spring of 1951, the national security issue of the moment centered on whether to expand an ongoing conflict in Korea by launching a large-scale bombing offensive targeting major cities in mainland China. From his headquarters in Tokyo, General Douglas MacArthur as commander in chief, Far East, was urging that course. General Omar Bradley, then chairing the Joint Chiefs of Staff, disagreed. Doing so, he told Congress, would involve the United States in "the wrong war, at the wrong place, at the wrong time, and with the wrong enemy." Although Bradley possessed little of MacArthur's charisma or capacity for histrionics, his advice prevailed. He thereby helped avert a strategic misstep and moral blunder of mammoth proportions.

What the events of 2020 revealed is this: Since 9/11, the United States has engaged in wars that General Bradley would have recognized as misguided and largely irrelevant, with actual threats to the safety and well-being of the American people treated as afterthoughts. In the third decade of the twenty-first century, the United States finds itself badly needing some Bradley Wisdom.

Indeed, since the fall of the Berlin Wall, such wisdom has been in short supply. Officials responsible for national security have repeatedly chosen to engage in "the wrong war, at the wrong place, at the wrong time, and with the wrong enemy." More accurately, they have chosen to engage in several wars in several places over the course of many years against several enemies. Unfortunately, no one of Bradley's stature has emerged to denounce the folly that has ensued. And no one has proven capable of formulating an alternative approach to basic policy that addresses the constellation of dangers that actually threaten the United States.

Misconstruing the Threat

Anyone wishing to understand the frailties and foibles of the human species should begin at the beginning: the story of Adam and Eve in the Garden. Anyone seeking to understand the cumulative deficiencies of U.S. national security policy in recent decades should begin with the phrase itself: *national security*.

Subsuming and going well beyond national defense, the concept of national security emerged during World War II and grew to maturity during the Cold War. National defense *had* meant something specific and concrete: protecting the American people where they live. National security implied far greater ambitions. Its defining feature was elasticity. Depending on circumstance, it could mean many things, even incorporating intangibles like *prestige* and *credibility*.

As national security supplanted national defense, protecting the American people was demoted to the status of a lesser concern. When it came to designing and deploying U.S. forces, other priorities took precedence. The perceived imperatives of national security during the Cold War provided a rationale for raising up immense nuclear forces, permanently garrisoning Western Europe with large troop contingents, and fighting costly wars in Korea and Vietnam. Mere national defense would never have sufficed to justify the many billions expended on each of these undertakings. Each was sold as contributing to a broader purpose.

Indeed, almost anything could be justified as long as it was linked to the phrase "national security." Consider National Security Action Memorandum (NSAM) 115, dated February 2, 1962, Subject: Defoliant Operations in Vietnam. Within the administration of John F. Kennedy, NSAMs—there would be 272 in all—translated general policy into specific actions. They were decision papers. Calling them National Security Action Memoranda—the Kennedy administration fancied itself as all about *action*—endowed them with an extra cachet of urgency and importance. And nowhere was the demand for action greater than in relation to any matter that touched on national security.

In 1962, U.S. involvement in the Vietnam War was still limited. But a quiet process of escalation was well under way, with civilian and military officials keen to identify low-cost "techniques and gadgets," as one army general put it, that might enhance the ongoing war effort.[6] The purpose of NSAM 115 was to get the president to approve a proposal to disperse herbicides across large swaths of South Vietnam and thereby gain an edge over the Communist insurgents.[7] Aerial spraying to kill plant life seemed to fit the bill.

In that sense, NSAM 115 represented just one more incremental expansion of the ongoing U.S. military campaign. JFK's chief advisers welcomed this prospect. Secretary of State Dean Rusk opined that "successful plant-killing operations" would be "of substantial assistance in the control and defeat of the Viet Cong." Secretary of Defense Robert McNamara saw real benefit in targeting "the subsistence available to the Viet Cong insurgents . . . by spraying their manioc, corn, sweet potato, rice, and other crops." In a memo to the president, McNamara's deputy Roswell Gilpatric offered assurances that "the agents have no harmful effects on humans, livestock, or soil. Their only effect is to kill the plant growth upon which sprayed." In the worst case, should "friendlies" such as Montagnard tribesmen suffer harmful effects, they could be moved, involuntarily. Here, it seemed, was a very clever idea, with few evident downsides.

More hesitant was Edward R. Murrow, the famous journalist who had enlisted in JFK's New Frontier to run the United States Information Agency. In a memo to national security adviser McGeorge Bundy, Murrow called attention to a series of articles by Rachel Carson then running in the *New Yorker* and destined to form the basis for her pathbreaking book *Silent Spring*. According to Murrow, the articles illustrated "with devastating impact the consequences of insecticide on insect-plant balance and human life." Murrow's immediate concern was the potentially adverse impact that a large-scale campaign of defoliation might have on America's image abroad. "I am persuaded that we cannot persuade the world—particularly that large part of it that does not get enough to eat—that defoliation is 'good for you.'"[8] But Morrow was not a member of JFK's inner circle and his tepid dissent was ignored.

So began Operation Ranch Hand, destined to continue from 1962 to 1971—its mordant but unofficial motto "Only You Can Prevent a Forest." Second only to the nuclear policy of Massive Retaliation, Ranch Hand may well qualify as the ultimate expression of the mindlessness to which the Cold War–inspired perversion of national security gave rise. Relying primarily on specially modified C-123 transport aircraft, the air force proceeded to dump some nineteen million gallons of various herbicides, Agent Orange being the most common, over an estimated six million acres of South Vietnam and Laos.[9]

Measured quantitatively, Ranch Hand was a great success— U.S. forces transformed great stretches of Indochina into barren

wasteland. Yet the operation had no discernible effect on the outcome of the war. Its impact on the Vietnamese people, however,
proved to be profound and lasting. Agent Orange and other
defoliants took the lives of an estimated four hundred thousand
Vietnamese, while adversely affecting the health of up to three
million more. The poisons spread across the landscape survived long after the war, contributing to an enormous spike
in birth defects and to the increased prevalence of various can-
cers. Americans who served in Vietnam also suffered ill effects
attributable to Ranch Hand. For example, the high incidence of
prostate cancer among Vietnam veterans (myself included) has
been traced to their probable exposure to Agent Orange.[10] Like
the Vietnam War as a whole, Ranch Hand proved to be a political and moral disaster.

Of course, the senior officials in the Kennedy administration who signed off on the use of herbicides in Vietnam and
the senior commanders in Saigon who implemented Operation Ranch Hand anticipated none of this. The conception of
national security to which they subscribed took human mastery over the natural world for granted. Apart from occasional
interruptions—Southeast Asia was periodically subjected to
monsoon rains, for example—nature was expected to accommo-
date the fascination with "techniques and gadgets" to which
policymakers and soldiers alike were susceptible. So while nature
might not be entirely compliant, it was inconceivable that once
used as a depository for toxins the natural world could become a
source of danger at least as menacing as anything the Viet Cong
were capable of devising.

Drawing on the insights of Rachel Carson, Murrow, alone
among JFK's advisers, came close to grasping what was to
become a crucially important truth: The punishment that nature

is capable of absorbing has limits; to exceed those limits is to endanger the safety and well-being of the human species. In short, if sufficiently abused, nature itself becomes the threat, with modernity potentially put at risk.

Throughout the remainder of the twentieth century and into the twenty-first, few national security officials were willing to take this prospect seriously. The dubious logic that produced Operation Ranch Hand survived. If anything, the conviction that "techniques and gadgets" held the key to national security became even more deeply entrenched. Washington continued to pay more attention to illusory threats in faraway places than to actual threats imperiling Americans where they live.

Slogans and Catchphrases

Basic national security policy emerged remarkably intact from the trauma of Vietnam. While the end of the war produced much anguished discussion about what "lessons" it had to teach, the moral and environmental implications of Operation Ranch Hand did not qualify for inclusion.

After a brief moment when the so-called Vietnam Syndrome produced hesitation to use force, normalcy returned. Saigon fell in 1975. By 1980, President Jimmy Carter had already identified the Persian Gulf, with its massive oil reserves, as a theater requiring U.S. military presence and action. Under the terms of this Carter Doctrine, preparations for war there began immediately.[11] In 1981, Ronald Reagan became president and initiated a major buildup of U.S. forces including, among other things, authorizing construction of the USS *Theodore Roosevelt*. A new generation of gadgets and techniques soon proliferated—weaponry, doctrines, and training methods.[12]

A series of small-scale overt and covert interventions in Lebanon, Libya, Grenada, El Salvador, and Nicaragua soon followed. By the mid-1980s, the symbiotic relationship between the Cold War and national security activism—each sustaining the other—was fully restored.

At which point, with the Soviet economy stagnant and the Red Army's decade-long military effort to pacify Afghanistan having failed (thanks in part to U.S. support for the Afghan resistance), the Kremlin decided to call the whole thing off. In late 1989, the Berlin Wall fell and the "long twilight struggle" abruptly ended. In theory, this astonishing turn of events might have prompted policymakers in Washington to rethink and replace the prevailing national security paradigm. No such rethinking occurred. The U.S. military, its prestige and political standing now fully restored to pre-Vietnam levels, exerted itself to preempt any such possibility.

At this juncture, an oracle spoke. Just as the Cold War was drawing to a close, NASA scientist James Hansen testified before the U.S. Senate Committee on Energy and Natural Resources. In brief remarks, Hansen invited the attention of committee members to "three main conclusions":

> Number one, the earth is warmer in 1988 than at any time in the history of instrumental measurements. Number two, the global warming is now large enough that we can ascribe with a high degree of confidence a cause and effect relationship to the greenhouse effect. And number three, our computer climate simulations indicate that the greenhouse effect is already large enough to begin to effect the probability of extreme events such as summer heat waves.[13]

According to the *New York Times*, Dr. Hansen's provocative testimony "sounded the alarm with such authority and force that the issue of an overheating world has suddenly moved to the forefront of public concern."[14] Unfortunately, the reporter's conclusion was itself wildly overheated. Hansen's findings did attract notice. But when it came to basic national security policy, he wielded less clout than Edward R. Murrow had in 1962. Those responsible for formulating post–Cold War strategy were no more attuned to the potential implications of climate change than were Kennedy's "best and brightest" to the consequences of Ranch Hand. Climate was not a matter that they found particularly relevant or even interesting.

What interested them instead was a careful redefinition of purpose designed to avert substantive change and forestall any diversion of resources from the national security apparatus. The idea was to tweak basic policy while preserving its essentials. As a result, a military establishment primarily intended to deter and defend now became an instrument of power projection.

The January 1992 version of the *National Military Strategy of the United States* (NMS) offered a justification for this reorientation. Published under the aegis of General Colin Powell, then serving as chairman of the Joint Chiefs of Staff, the 1992 NMS appeared barely a month after the dissolution of the Soviet Union and less than a year after Operation Desert Storm had ended in a seemingly decisive coalition victory over Iraq. According to Powell, the new strategy contained "a number of departures from principles that have shaped the American defense posture since the Second World War." As if cribbed directly from Kennedy's New Frontier, the new principles emphasized action.

Most significant is the shift from containing the spread
of communism and deterring Soviet aggression to a more
diverse, flexible strategy that is regionally oriented and
capable of responding decisively to the challenges of this
decade.

"Forward Presence" and "Crisis Response" comprised the cor-
nerstones of this new strategy. Keeping U.S. forces "deployed
throughout the world" would demonstrate "commitment, lend
credibility to our alliances, enhance regional stability, and provide a crisis response capability." Forward presence and crisis
response went hand in glove. Taken together, they would enable
the United States to deal with any problems that might crop up
anywhere on the planet, keeping Americans safe and enabling
them to enjoy freedom.[15]

While the disappearance of the Soviet Empire made it difficult to identify those threats with any specificity, the NMS
pointed to "the intensification of intractable conflicts between
historic enemies" as a concern, along with nuclear proliferation,
drug trafficking, and "the continuing struggle to improve the
human condition throughout the world." Worst of all were the
dangers beyond the ken of Pentagon planners: "The real threat
we now face is the threat of the unknown, the uncertain." In
sum, as it ventured into that uncertain future, the U.S. military
would surely have plenty of work to do.

The 1992 NMS did not mention the possibility of nature
itself posing a problem. In the Pentagon, Dr. Hansen's warning went unheeded, as it did again in the 1995 NMS. Under
the heading of "Transnational Dangers," that document made
passing mention of disease, but without proposing a plan of

action.[16] Climate per se went unmentioned, as it would in the subsequent editions of the *National Military Strategy* published in 1997, 2004, and 2015. When in response to congressional prodding, the Pentagon finally got around to assessing the "National Security Implications of Climate-Related Risks and a Changing Climate" in 2015, its report avoided specifics and conveyed no sense of urgency. The various military commands were "beginning to include the implications of a changing climate in its frameworks for managing operational and strategic risks prudently."[17] Congress was going to have to be satisfied with that.

Successive versions of the NMS featured slogans or catchphrases, accompanied by colorful graphics, all intended to reassure one and all that the U.S. military was fully cognizant of how the global security environment was changing. In 1995, the organizing theme was "Shared Situational Awareness; Real Time Forces Synchronization"; in 1997, "Shape, Respond, Prepare";[18] in 2004, "Full Spectrum Dominance";[19] in 2015, "hybrid conflict."[20] For the most part, this was jargon devised to conceal the absence of critical thinking.

In fairness, especially during the long wars that followed 9/11, the here and now gave the U.S. military more than enough to deal with. With its hands full just countering IEDs and rooting out insurgents, the Pentagon had little institutional bandwidth left for imagining a future that might drastically differ from what they were familiar with. As a consequence, military planners overlooked or chose to ignore signs of change at odds with their existing preconceptions. They clung tightly to the conviction that, if adequately funded, the armed forces of the United States were more than capable of ensuring American safety and prosperity. The generals and admirals in charge were like manufacturers of buggy whips and horse-drawn wagons at the dawn of the automobile age.

This does not mean that the armed services were standing still. The army, navy, and air force (less so the Marine Corps) were more or less continuously engaged in recapitalizing, which in practice meant replacing aging machines with improved and updated versions of the same thing—better tanks, better fighter planes, better long-range bombers. To cite but one example, in November 2009, the keel was laid on the navy's latest class of aircraft carriers. With construction to continue until 2058, the USS *Gerald Ford* and other ships in its class, ten in all, will replace the *Nimitz*-class ships. (When the fifth *Ford*-class carrier joins the fleet, the *Theodore Roosevelt* will retire.) Including cost overruns, the *Ford*'s price tag exceeds $13.7 billion, not counting the cost of the aircraft it will carry.[21] Other ships in the class will inevitably cost even more. Given a warship's expected useful life span, the navy is counting on *Ford*-class carriers to ply the high seas and conduct air strikes until roughly the end of the twenty-first century.

As anyone who has visited a modern aircraft carrier (or watched the movie *Top Gun*) will attest, these are magnificent machines, throwbacks to an era when the United States made the finest of whatever there was to make. But as suggested by the *Theodore Roosevelt* taking sanctuary in Guam as the COVID-19 pandemic was exploding, these artifacts retain questionable relevance to the emerging security environment. This describes exactly the problem facing the U.S. military as a whole.

For the officers who lead that military, imbued since the day of their commissioning with the conviction that theirs is the mightiest armed force in all of history, even to hint that their services might verge on becoming superfluous is tantamount to blasphemy. For elected officials, especially those with major weapons contractors located in their home districts, any such suggestion is similarly intolerable. To patriotic citizens schooled in the belief that the officials responsible for shaping basic national security policy know what they are doing, the very idea that U.S. forces might be waging war against the wrong enemy in the wrong place is almost inconceivable—at least it was until COVID-19 caught those officials entirely off guard.

As far back as World War II, the term "threat," when used in a national security context, connoted immediate and existential danger, with first Nazi Germany and then the nuclear-armed Soviet Union as primary examples. Even when the Cold War ended, the term retained that connotation, despite the fact that adversaries now classified as threats posed dangers that were neither immediate nor existential. No matter: The old usage persisted, mere accuracy taking a backseat to utility as a vehicle for scaremongering and justifying copious funding for the Pentagon.

During the 1990s, with no adversary comparable to the Soviet Union immediately at hand, the Pentagon devised the phrase "rogue nation" to serve as a generic threat, with Saddam Hussein's Iraq the preferred illustrative example.[22] After 9/11, "rogue nation" fell out of favor. Drawing on memories of World War II, George W. Bush created out of whole cloth an Axis of Evil, with Iran and North Korea now joining Iraq to comprise the threat. Today, twenty years later, with Iraq merely a mess rather than a source of danger, Iran retains a place on Washington's semiofficial threat roster, as does North Korea. Yet that roster has now undergone further expansion, with post-Soviet Russia and the People's Republic of China recent additions.

What is the common denominator shared by these various threats to U.S. national security? Crucially, they are nation-states and they are far away. Adhering to Colin Powell's three-decades-old prescription, they qualify as what we might call *Pentagon-preferred adversaries*, their very existence justifying a military establishment that is still configured to project power against distant enemies.

Here we arrive at the abiding, unspoken premise of basic U.S. policy, spanning both the Cold War and all the years since: the conviction that containing or deterring or coercing nation-states that are both far away and classified as dangerous holds the key to keeping Americans safe at home and guaranteeing their freedom. The existence of such distant adversaries pro-vides the raison d'être for the *Theodore Roosevelt*, the *Gerald Ford*, and the entire national security state.

On occasion the United States has found itself face-to-face with threats that did not conform to the profile of Pentagon-preferred adversaries. On each such occasion, with the American people gripped by fear, the existing national security paradigm was found wanting.

The first occasion was the Cuban Missile Crisis, the second 9/11, and the third the coronavirus pandemic of 2020. Seem-ingly unrelated, these three episodes lay bare the inadequacies of the prevailing national security paradigm. As such, they have much to teach.

Located just ninety miles off the coast of Florida, Cuba is the very inverse of far away. During the early phases of the Cold War, pursuant to enabling Americans to sleep worry-free, suc-cessive administrations had amassed a vast arsenal of nuclear weapons while covertly subverting regimes not to Washington's liking. Between 1947 when the Cold War was just getting under way and 1961 when John F. Kennedy became president, the nation's nuclear stockpile had increased from thirteen to an astonishing twenty-three thousand warheads.[23] That same year, a Kennedy-approved CIA plan to overthrow Cuba's Communist leader Fidel Castro by landing counterrevolutionaries at the Bay of Pigs backfired ignominiously. Eighteen months later, Washington's mindless accumulation of nuclear weapons and penchant for covert operations combined to produce the Cuban Missile Crisis.

In effect, Washington's preoccupation with faraway threats yielded a genuinely dangerous one right at the nation's back door. While U.S. military commanders were fully prepared to do what they had done a decade earlier to North Korea and would soon do to North Vietnam—bomb Cuba to smithereens—Kennedy concluded that using force to eliminate Soviet nuclear weapons in Cuba could well result in something much worse: World War III. So he backed away from the abyss. His secret negotiations with Soviet leader Nikita Khrushchev avoided Armageddon and reduced Cuba to a mere nuisance. In other words, when an existential threat actually materialized, the prevailing national security paradigm had proven irrelevant. By discarding its premises and cutting a deal with the Kremlin, Kennedy saved the nation and arguably all of humankind.

A second instance revealing the shortcomings of that paradigm relates to al-Qaeda, which, most inconveniently for the U.S. national security apparatus, was not a nation-state. Instead, it was a terrorist organization of impressive reach and durability.[24] Even so, when 9/11 prompted Congress to *declare* war on terrorism, the George W. Bush administration opted to *wage* war against readily available Pentagon-preferred adversaries, even those with no direct involvement in the attacks on the World Trade Center and the Pentagon.

That this made no sense strategically soon became evident. If nothing else, the ensuing campaigns in Afghanistan and Iraq testified to how deeply ingrained the existing national security paradigm had become. The Bush administration's fixation on threats in faraway nation-states overrode all other considerations. So the troops gamely went off and did what they were trained, organized, and equipped to do. The ensuing wars, long or endless or forever, represented the ultimate disregard for General Bradley's famous dictum.

It remained for COVID-19 once and for all to truly drive home the shortcomings of the existing national security paradigm. In 2020, pursuant to that paradigm, the United States was spending approximately a trillion dollars per year.[25] As the coronavirus pandemic ravaged the nation, that lavish expenditure of resources was all but irrelevant to the problem at hand.

The Department of Defense did mobilize a pair of hospital ships that made a token contribution to treating the sick in New York and Los Angeles.[26] State governors ordered small contingents of National Guard troops to help erect temporary treatment facilities and perform support tasks. And the Air Force Thunderbirds and the Navy's Blue Angels conducted flyovers of major cities to express the Pentagon's appreciation for the gallantry of medical personnel and first responders.[27] The gestures might have been appreciated. But their substantive value was negligible.

Ranch Hand Writ Large

From a national security perspective, the coronavirus pandemic posed some crucial questions. Does all the frenetic activity of U.S. forces as they prepare for and wage war in faraway places contribute to keeping Americans safe at home? Or does it distract from that purpose? Is all of the money consumed annually by the national security establishment enhancing our collective welfare? Or are these expenditures merely diverting resources from priorities of greater relevance to the well-being of the American people?

Answering those questions requires revising our understanding of what constitutes a threat. To judge by what actually kills or dispossesses Americans, undermines their economic prosperity, and compromises their freedoms, faraway nation-states pose less of a danger than deformities in the natural world caused by human activity.

When I lie awake at night worrying about the planet that my grandchildren will inherit, it's not terrorism that prevents me from sleeping. Nor is it Iran or North Korea or Russia or even China. It's the puerile witlessness of a national security apparatus oblivious to real and proximate dangers that, if ignored, will only worsen with time and ultimately jeopardize the American way of life. It's non-Pentagon-preferred threats typically treated as addenda that demand our attention.

Those threats come in three distinct forms. First are short-duration catastrophes, misleadingly referred to as natural disasters or even more misleadingly as acts of God. These include storms, floods, and wildfires, all of them intensifying in their severity as a direct result of climate change.[28]

The second threat is cumulative rather than episodic. It comes in the form of resource depletion disastrously affecting soil, water, wildlife, and the quality of the air we breathe. These, too, stem directly from human activity.[29] The extinction of animal species offers an especially vivid example of the consequences, as does the presence of microplastic particles in what is ostensibly ocean-caught fresh seafood sold in American markets.[30] Then there are the droughts, which are becoming more frequent, more severe, and longer lasting.[31]

And finally, there are infectious diseases, with COVID-19 a representative but hardly unique example. Since 1981, the HIV epidemic has taken the lives of some seven hundred thousand Americans.[32] Here, too, in some instances, climate change can be a factor, fostering the spread of vectors and exacerbating the severity of outbreaks, with SARS in 2003 and Ebola in 2014–2016 as recent examples.[33]

While still controversial in quarters where climate change is treated as fiction, such threats are real and continue to produce punishing effects. Consider the toll in recent years from massively powerful hurricanes. In 2005, Katrina caused $125 billion in damage. In 2012, came Sandy: $75 billion. Twenty seventeen proved to be a banner year with Hurricanes Harvey ($125 billion), Irma ($65 billion), and Maria ($91 billion) occurring within a two-month period. These financial figures do not include the hundreds killed, thousands injured, and tens of thousands left homeless.[34]

Had such devastating losses resulted from enemy attack, Americans would have had no difficulty in situating them under the heading of national security failures, much like Pearl Harbor or 9/11. As it is, they are written off as misfortunes that fall beyond the writ of our trillion-dollar-per-annum national security apparatus. For any threat to which there is no obvious military response, the national security state gives itself a pass—the equivalent of a fire department refusing to respond to any emergency unless smoke and flames are evident.

The problem here is one of definition: A narrow conception of national security satisfies the needs of the armed forces and the military-industrial complex. It also works nicely for elected officials in hock to weapons makers. But that cramped conception leaves the American people vulnerable to whatever misfortune befalls them next. Such misfortunes are arriving with increasing frequency and ever greater severity. Meanwhile, the obvious solutions—more thorough advanced preparation, improved warning, faster and more effective response, and hastening the transition to a post–fossil fuel economy—languish. Replacing *Nimitz*-class nuclear aircraft carriers rates as a far higher (and more lucrative) priority.

What we have here, in other words, are the lessons of Operation Ranch Hand writ large. Today the American fascination with "techniques and gadgets" knows no bounds. Expectations that we can oblige nature to do our bidding survive, even as mounting evidence shows that those efforts are producing acute and perhaps irreversible harm. In terms of strategic prescience, Rachel Carson turned out to be light-years ahead of Kennedy's men and all those "best and brightest" who have followed in the decades since.

What Carson glimpsed in the early 1960s has now become plainly evident: To preserve the American way of life will require curbing its excesses. The countless decisions, large and small, made over the course of a century or more that define freedom in terms of indulging our appetite for consumption, mobility, and unlimited choice have created threats more dangerous than any faraway nation-state.[35] We have become our own worst enemy.

And neither the *Theodore Roosevelt* nor the rest of the national security apparatus can save us.

6

WHY WE FOUGHT/WHY WE FIGHT

Race subverts America's self-assigned role as the champion of freedom. It did so in 1776 and it does so still today. "How is it," the English writer Samuel Johnson wondered as the colonists in British North America pressed their demands for independence, "that the loudest yelps for liberty come from the drivers of slaves?"

The question is one that most white Americans, especially those occupying positions of political authority, have sought to evade. For a remarkably long period of time, they succeeded in doing so, chiefly by styling any exercise of power by the United States as advancing the cause of freedom everywhere. In that context, it became necessary to ignore or conceal the fact that more than a few Americans were themselves denied freedom.

The series of World War II documentaries called *Why We Fight* offers a notable instance of this time-honored practice. Soon after Pearl Harbor, the War Department commissioned Frank Capra, a famous movie director then in uniform, to create the series, which Capra himself envisioned as a response to Leni Riefenstahl's infamous Nazi propaganda film *Triumph of the Will*.[1] Capra more than made good on his aim.

Awarded an Oscar for best documentary, *Why We Fight* was itself a propaganda masterpiece. Capra's sequence of seven films seamlessly blended a sanitized interpretation of American history with a greatly simplified account of the origins of World War II. The history describes a people deeply devoted to liberty and equality for all, who wish for nothing more than to live in peace. The account of the war's origins recounts the nation's slow awakening to the imperative of fighting to ensure freedom's very survival. The process was slow because, as the narrator in episode one intones, "We hadn't yet learned that peace for us depends on peace for all."[2] Only after December 7, 1941, did Americans realize that "this is a fight between a free world and a slave world," with the war to destroy Nazi Germany, Fascist Italy, and Imperial Japan "a common man's life and death struggle against those who would put him back in slavery."[3]

As to the historical reality of American slavery and its legacy, Capra's series maintained a studied silence. Indeed, it barely acknowledged the existence of Americans who were not white and ethnically European. Taken as a whole, *Why We Fight* all but ignored race, notwithstanding the prevailing reality of de jure segregation throughout the South and de facto segregation throughout much of the North.

Yet mobilizing the nation for total war necessarily meant mobilizing African Americans, too. Some 1.2 million Black soldiers would, in fact, serve in the U.S. military during World War II, the vast majority of them draftees—this at a time when, for many white Americans, their Black fellow citizens did not fully qualify as part of *we*. It became incumbent upon the War Department, therefore, to explain why *they* should fight.

To address this requirement, Capra produced an addendum to his series, which the War Department released in 1944 as *The Negro Soldier*. Some forty-seven minutes in length, the film was itself a remarkable document.

Set in a stately church filled to capacity with an all-Black congregation of well-dressed men and women, *The Negro Soldier* employed a series of staged flashbacks to recount the history of Black Americans as a narrative of unbroken heroic service in American wars dating from the Revolution—while avoiding any reference to the Civil War.[4] Neither slavery nor post-Emancipation serfdom qualified for mention. Yet in a sharp departure from Hollywood's typical rendering of Black Americans as either servile, dim-witted, or with talents limited to singing and dancing, the African American community depicted in *The Negro Soldier* consisted of devout, prosperous, contented, and patriotic citizens.

The pastor, effectively the film's narrator, begins the service by recalling the 1938 prizefight in which Joe Louis knocked out the German Max Schmeling in the first round. Now, he tells his congregants, "the fight for the real championship of the world" has begun, with Joe Louis himself in the fight. (The poster advertising the movie featured a uniformed Private Louis wielding an M1 Garand rifle. The text read: "America's Joe Louis vs. the Axis!")[5] The pastor then proceeds to read aloud passages from *Mein Kampf* in which Adolf Hitler derides any effort to educate a Black person—"a born half-ape"—as "a sin against all reason" and "criminal madness."

The message is clear: Yes, racism exists, but its home is Nazi Germany, not the United States of America. The fight for the real championship of the world, therefore, is one in which all Black Americans should willingly do their part.

Capra's film does not dwell on how victory might affect African Americans. To judge from *The Negro Soldier*, their situation already rated as more than satisfactory. So while Blacks might be living apart from whites (and serving apart from them in a Jim Crow army), all shared in the freedom that defined the American way of life. Even if separate, they were substantively equal, as Capra's African Americans themselves appear to acknowledge and appreciate. Thus did a white moviemaker incorporate Blacks into his cinematic chronicle of Americans fighting for freedom.

All of this, of course, was a mirage, concocted in the best Hollywood tradition.

The Freedom Narrative Undone—and Renegotiated

In the American collective consciousness, the conflict enshrined by *Why We Fight* remains the definitive war for freedom. Even today, notwithstanding the impact of the Trump presidency, the coronavirus pandemic, painful economic recession, and Black Lives Matter, World War II still serves as a wellspring of national legitimacy, arguably surpassing that stemming from the Revolution and the Civil War.

Best of all, the conflict ended in total victory, the newspaper headlines on V-J Day proclaiming PEACE! The end of World War II did not give way to peace, however. Instead, a decades-long emergency almost immediately commenced, marked by further wars and innumerable crises, with Armageddon hovering in the shadows. With the coming of the Cold War, political leaders of both parties fell into the habit of privileging national security over all other concerns, including race. While not ignored, racial inequality became a problem to be managed rather than confronted. In the Congress, stalwart southern segregationists like Carl Vinson, John Stennis, and Richard Russell proved to be staunch Cold Warriors, courted by the Pentagon and subsequently honored as great statesmen.[6]

For African Americans, the onset of the Cold War imparted a further complicating twist to the question of *why we fight*. During World War II, the vile white racists who threatened freedom's very existence (the German ones, at least) demanded a response from all Americans, regardless of color. This was Capra's summons, with Black Americans by and large rising to the occasion. During the Cold War, however, U.S. forces went into battle against enemies who were neither white nor overtly racist.

What those new enemies shared in common was a professed affinity for Communism. From their own exposure to that ideology, however, politically aware African Americans knew that Communist dogma steadfastly rejected racism in whatever form. During the 1920s and 1930s, while Republicans and Democrats either affirmed or turned a blind eye to segregation, the Communist Party USA loudly proclaimed its commitment to racial equality.[7] More than a few leading lights of the Black intelligentsia, including W. E. B. Du Bois, Langston Hughes, Claude McKay, Paul Robeson, and Richard Wright, either joined the party or flirted with doing so.[8] From a Black perspective, the incompatibility of freedom and Marxism-Leninism was not immediately apparent.

Then, in the summer of 1950, the imperative of standing steadfast against Communism prompted the Truman administration to intervene in Korea. According to President Harry Truman, the U.S. forces hurriedly dispatched to authoritarian

South Korea were fighting for "liberty and peace."[9] This was at best an oversimplification. Framing the Korean War as another fight for freedom proved to be a tough sell, especially when an ill-advised allied counteroffensive into Communist North Korea brought the People's Republic of China into the conflict. The Korean "police action" had become longer and bloodier than Truman or the American people had expected.

That said, while never popular, the Korean War did improve the status of Black soldiers by putting an end to Jim Crow in the U.S. Army. Given the complexity of ensuring that some Black replacement didn't accidentally end up in a white rifle company, senior commanders in Korea decided that they might as well comply with President Truman's 1948 executive order to integrate the armed forces.

For the high command, integration stemmed less from a commitment to equality than from a desire to end administrative hassles and facilitate the assignment of soldiers based on skill rather than color.[10] During World War II, most "colored troops" had been assigned to service, i.e., noncombat, units. The hot wars of the Cold War now thrust Black soldiers into the front lines where they enjoyed opportunities to die for their country equal to that of their white compatriots.

Even so, with segregation still entrenched across the South and the Senate adamantly refusing even to pass an anti-lynching bill, it was difficult to make the case that Black soldiers fighting to keep South Korea "free" were thereby advancing the cause of Black freedom at home.[11] African American troops were now very much in the fray, but in comparison with World War II, *why* they were fighting had become shrouded in ambiguity.

Then came Vietnam, another episode that found GIs fighting in a distant country of dubious provenance and questionable democratic bona fides. By the 1960s, with integration of the enlisted ranks an accomplished fact, African American soldiers were overrepresented in combat units. (Black commissioned officers remained relatively few in number and Black generals all but nonexistent.)[12] As a consequence, once U.S. forces began deploying to Vietnam in large numbers, Black troops sustained a disproportionate number of casualties—nearly 25 percent of those killed during the first year of major combat.[13]

An uproar ensued. In response, the Pentagon hastened to implement policy changes so that Black losses would approximate their proportion of the force. Nonetheless, those early casualty figures created an indelible impression: In a war destined to become the most unpopular in all of U.S. history, African American troops were doing more than their fair share of the fighting and dying.

Vietnam resembled World War II in at least one important respect: Federal authorities still relied on conscription to put young Americans in uniform. Perpetuating a system of involuntary service demanded a persuasive answer to *why we fight* relevant to the case at hand. Efforts by government authorities to provide that answer came up short.[14] Soon enough, resistance to the draft, especially among privileged whites, became widespread. As increasing numbers of young white men finagled ways to avoid serving and as the reformist civil rights movement took a radical turn toward Black Power, persuading African Americans that they had a stake in Vietnam became a challenge. When Joe Louis received his induction orders in 1941, he readily complied. A quarter century later, when Muhammad Ali got his draft notice, he refused. "I ain't got no quarrel with them Vietcong," the Champ told reporters.[15]

The very next year, Martin Luther King mounted the pulpit

at Manhattan's Riverside Church to denounce a war that was taking "black young men who had been crippled by our society and sending them eight thousand miles away to guarantee liberties in Southeast Asia which they had not found in southwest Georgia and East Harlem."[16] Employing his immense moral authority, King validated convictions that were already finding purchase in many parts of American society and, perhaps more significantly, among Black GIs: Vietnam simply did not qualify as a fight for freedom.

Eldridge Cleaver of the Black Panther Party was even more direct. In his letter "To My Black Brothers in Vietnam," Cleaver wrote, "I know that you niggers have your minds all messed up about Black organizations, or you wouldn't be the flunkies for the white organization—the U.S.A.—for whom you have picked up the gun." The Panthers, he continued, had "picked up the gun too, but not to fight against the heroic Vietnamese people, but rather to wage war of liberation against the very same pigs whom you are helping to run their vicious game on the entire world, including your own people."[17] Cleaver urged Black GIs to do likewise.

As the war dragged on, active resistance by Black troops at home, in the war zone, and at other posts overseas became widespread.[18] Across the armed services discipline unraveled, catching political and military elites unawares.[19]

A pivotal moment in U.S. military history arrived. Prior to Vietnam, the African American contribution to the nation's wars had qualified as useful but less than essential. Now, that was changing. Vietnam soured many young Americans not only on serving in that particular war but on military service more generally. As young white males found increasingly inventive ways of giving war a wide berth—George W. Bush joined the

National Guard, Dick Cheney applied for a series of student deferments, Donald Trump complained of bone spurs—Black willingness to serve and to fight became indispensable. Were African Americans to join with whites in deciding that the United States was not worth fighting for, American military power, the preeminent expression of the nation's status as a global power, would wither.

The All-Volunteer Force created in response to the Nixon administration's 1970 decision to abandon conscription tacitly acknowledged the collapse of the government's authority to mandate military service. According to President Richard Nixon, "the unfairness of the present system" required its termination.[20] More accurately, that system was imploding, leaving federal authorities with little choice but to junk it. The AVF represented a crash effort to devise a replacement.

Making the AVF work required the Pentagon to implement comprehensive reforms designed to increase the appeal of military service to any able-bodied youngster recruiters could induce to enlist. This meant improving pay and benefits and reducing the everyday chickenshit that had long formed an intrinsic part of service life. Yet few doubted that the near-term prospects and long-term viability of the AVF depended on the willingness of Black kids from the projects to enlist. Recruiters counting on the children of white suburbia to fill the ranks of the army after Vietnam were in for a long wait. Yet making the AVF more attractive to prospective Black soldiers—a crucially important "market" for recruiters—required purging the nominally integrated services of any remaining vestiges of racism.

Improved opportunities for advancement offered a substantive measure of progress toward true equality. So the Pentagon worked hard to persuade Blacks that military service offered prospects for upward mobility not available in most other sectors of American life. With the creation of the AVF many more African Americans gained admission to West Point, Annapolis, and the Air Force Academy.[21] More achieved promotion to the rank of general or admiral. Scholars took note, citing the armed forces as "the only place in America where blacks routinely boss around whites."[22] This defined the new compact between African Americans and the U.S. military, one to which a grateful political establishment, eager for the soldiery to return to its traditional compliant and politically inert status, gave full assent.

Reduced to its essence, the new arrangement had two tacit provisos. According to the first, white political elites, their ranks now including a smattering of Blacks, would continue to direct basic national security policy, deciding when and where it was necessary to fight. According to the second, actual combat fell under the jurisdiction of a racially mixed force that was disproportionately Black.

In 1989, when President George H. W. Bush nominated General Colin Powell, a Black officer, to the post of chairman of the Joint Chiefs of Staff—the Senate voting unanimously to confirm his appointment—that new deal reached an apotheosis of sorts.[23] Powell was Barack Obama before Obama: cool, confident, and telegenic. His elevation to the very top of the military hierarchy seemingly proved that within the U.S. military, if nowhere else in American society, racial equality was now an accomplished fact.

Coming just two years later, Operation Desert Storm invested this apparent fact with even larger significance when Powell took it upon himself to explain what this latest war signified. In doing so, he asserted a prerogative hitherto reserved for whites. It was akin to the First Lady suddenly mounting the rostrum to deliver the State of the Union address.

Just weeks after the Gulf War, Powell addressed the annual policy conference of the American Israel Public Affairs Committee (AIPAC)—an unusual venue for a serving officer—to explain what had occurred. "In their heroism on the battlefield, and in their selfless sacrifice," Powell told those in attendance, the GIs who fought in the Gulf had "shown the world what America is all about." This largest campaign since Vietnam confirmed that the nation was now back on track.

> Desert Storm has demonstrated that the United States remains a superpower. I do not say this to gloat, I state this as a fact. What does it mean to be a superpower? It means being there when the alarm goes off. When our friends call in distress America does not put them on hold. Indeed, if we do our job well those calls may never have to be made.[24]

As in World War II, the United States was once more a liberator. As during the Cold War, it was once again the keeper of the peace. By citing the Gulf War as a demonstration of "what America is all about," however, Powell was doing much more than giving the troops a pat on the back. He was putting his personal seal of approval on claims of American Exceptionalism—that America was both unique and uniquely called upon to lead the world.

This was the language of white elites.

At his retirement ceremony on September 30, 1993, Powell revisited these themes. "The aspiring nations of the world trust the United States," he told an audience of admirers.

They need the United States. They need our political leadership. They need our economic strength. They need our value system as a model to learn from. They need our military strength. They need our military commitment to help keep order and to help prevent aggression.[25]

This, too, was the language of white elites.

From its very beginnings, America's ascent to power had been primarily a white undertaking. Visionary, ambitious, even ruthless white men—presidents, generals, explorers, pioneers, industrialists—had conceived of and directed the nation's growth. As the United States expanded, accrued strength, and created wealth on a staggering scale, white citizens had been the principal beneficiaries. Now the most influential and visible Black military officer in all of U.S. history was endorsing that project. Here was an explanation of *why we fight* that all Americans, regardless of color, could embrace as their own.

In many quarters of American life, race remained and would remain a source of contention. But as far as the nation's role in a post–Cold War world was concerned—global hegemony marketed as benign leadership—race had seemingly been put to rest. This defined General Powell's principal legacy, destined within barely more than a decade to yield poisonous fruit.

Why We Fight Wars That Never End

As was the case with Barack Obama's election to the presidency in 2008, appearances belied a more complex reality. In the immediate wake of the Gulf War, notwithstanding Powell's optimistic predictions, alarms began sounding and never ceased. Responding to those alarms kept the troops on the go, not only in the Persian Gulf but also in the Horn of Africa, the Balkans, and Central Asia. Mere days after Powell's retirement, in an episode subsequently enshrined as "Black Hawk Down," a contingent of army rangers sustained a small but costly defeat at the hands of Somali militants who did not view the United States as "a model to learn from." Powell's expectation that "if we do our job well those calls may never have to be made" remained a pipe dream.

General Powell's term as Joint Chiefs chairman occurred at a pivotal point in American military history. During the early 1990s, the United States embarked willy-nilly upon a decades-long period of hyper-interventionism. At least until the trying spring and summer of 2020, the signature event of this period occurred in 2003, when the United States initiated a war of choice targeting Iraq. As the centerpiece of the Global War on Terrorism launched in response to 9/11, the Iraq War remains the source of considerable controversy. Yet from our post-Trump/ post-COVID/Black Lives Matter perspective, a particularly relevant aspect of that war was this one: Operation Iraqi Freedom represented a desperate effort to preserve the authority and credibility of the "wise men" accustomed to presiding over the national security establishment—this at a time when "wise" was still largely synonymous with white and male.

The wise men had enjoyed a remarkable run. In the immediate wake of World War II, eminences such as soldier-statesman George C. Marshall, Secretary of State Dean Acheson, and Secretary of Defense Robert Lovett had been "present at the creation" of an entirely new conception of national security.[26] Without exception, the senior officials who determined the course of U.S. policy during the early years of the Cold War were cut from the same cloth and had the same skin color.

By the 1960s, a successor generation, with Dean Rusk, Robert McNamara, and McGeorge Bundy as leading lights, went badly astray as they justified and directed the nation's descent into the agonies of Vietnam. A slightly chastened cohort, which included luminaries such as Henry Kissinger, Zbigniew Brzezinski, George Shultz, and Brent Scowcroft, succeeded in reconstituting American power after Vietnam. In doing so, they also restored the collective authority of their highly credentialed and self-selecting clan.

With Colin Powell the token Black admitted to their ranks, they also revived a sense of American assertiveness badly damaged by Vietnam, a point driven home when U.S. forces sent to the Persian Gulf "kicked the Vietnam syndrome once and for all."[27] Combined with the fall of the Berlin Wall in 1989, the Gulf War elevated the prestige of the national security mandarins to new heights. No need for ordinary citizens to worry about national security or America's safety or standing in the world: Members of an almost exclusively white policy elite had things well in hand.

The events of 9/11 caught members of this elite napping, although none owned up to sleeping on duty. To conceal their collective dereliction (which was also his own), President George W. Bush framed the moment in terms reminiscent of Frank Capra. On September 20, 2001, Bush appeared before a Joint Session of Congress to denounce the attackers. "We have seen their kind before," he declared.

> They are the heirs of all the murderous ideologies of the 20th century. By sacrificing human life to serve their radical visions—by abandoning every value except the will to power—they follow in the path of fascism, and Nazism,

and totalitarianism. And they will follow that path all the way, to where it ends: in history's unmarked grave of discarded lies.[28]

It was World War II all over again. There was no need to ask *why we fight*. The question answered itself: 9/11 had inaugurated a new fight for freedom, the moment calling not for reflection but for doing what needed to be done.

With the World Trade Center still smoldering, men fancying themselves the heirs of Marshall, Acheson, and Lovett began pressing for the United States to invade Iraq. Endorsing that prospect was a platoon of influential media figures, also white. Prominent in the former category were Vice President Dick Cheney and Defense Secretary Donald Rumsfeld, along with Rumsfeld's deputy Paul Wolfowitz. Prominent in the latter category were David Brooks and Thomas Friedman of the *New York Times*; Richard Cohen of the *Washington Post*; Christopher Hitchens of *Vanity Fair*; Max Boot, Robert Kagan, and William Kristol of the *Weekly Standard*; Rich Lowry of the *National Review*; George Packer of the *New Yorker*; and the blogger Andrew Sullivan. The urge to oust Saddam Hussein from power, despite the absence of any concrete evidence linking the Iraqi dictator to the attacks on New York and Washington, had an unmistakable racial tint.

Iraq was, in sum, a white man's war. The officials who dreamed it up were white.[29] So, too, were the journalists who as de facto propagandists labored to sell the war to the American public. Differing on many other issues, these nominal antagonists—the one group wielding power, the other charged with holding the powerful accountable—were as one in arguing for employing force to uphold a conception of America's purpose to which they unanimously subscribed.

That conception of purpose, responding to History's putative summons to exercise unquestioned global leadership, did not arise from the offspring of former slaves. Neither was it the handiwork of Native Americans, Mexican migrants, or Asian laborers. The graduates of Harvard, Princeton, Yale, and West Point who traditionally presided over the American Empire understood it to be a white enterprise. While non-whites might be called upon to *wage* war on behalf of that empire, white Americans had always *directed* it.

Senior officials like Cheney, Rumsfeld, and Wolfowitz instantly realized that 9/11 posed a threat not only to that empire but also to their own authority. Their place in the political cosmos rested entirely on the claim that they possessed special knowledge essential to keeping America safe. Now the attack on New York and Washington had exposed that claim as utterly specious. Their egregious failure had put at risk the accumulated credibility carefully built up by their predecessors going back generations. As a consequence, the entire edifice of national security—the panoply of arrangements that installed men like Cheney, Rumsfeld, and Wolfowitz in positions of power—was teetering.

So whether or not Saddam actually had any real connection to al-Qaeda—he didn't—was beside the point. Anything less than a forceful response and U.S. claims to global primacy would become tenuous. So, too, would their own professional standing. Employing overwhelming military power to eliminate Saddam would once more show "the world what America is all about," while not so incidentally shoring up the status of the senior officials whom Osama bin Laden had caught asleep at the switch.

It fell to Colin Powell to facilitate their efforts. Doing so cost him his reputation.

A Black Man Takes the Fall

By nature, Powell had an aversion to risk. Now, as secretary of state during George W. Bush's first term, he entertained serious misgivings about invading Saddam Hussein's Iraq. As a former soldier, he was alert to the potentially negative consequences, both military and diplomatic, if the war did not unfold as planned. As the nation's chief diplomat, he worried that those consequences would be worse still if the United States acted without the prior assent of the UN Security Council.[30]

The first generation of wise men in the late 1940s and early 1950s had professed respect for the United Nations. This latest generation tended to see the world body as an irritant. With or without Security Council approval, they intended to use Iraq as a venue for making a statement: To defy America was to invite certain destruction. So only with reluctance did the Bush administration agree to go through the motions of seeking UN authorization.

Coaxing the world to allow the United States to play by its own rules promised to be difficult. But if anyone could persuade the Security Council to acquiesce in the looming U.S. invasion of Iraq, thereby implementing the recently promulgated Bush Doctrine of preventive war, Powell seemed the man for the job.[31] As a reluctant warrior with a rock-solid reputation for integrity, he would at the very least receive a serious hearing. In the halls of the thoroughly diverse United Nations, his racial identity only added to his standing.[32]

On February 5, 2003, Powell appeared before the Security Council (and a worldwide television audience) to argue that Iraq represented a grave and imminent threat to international peace and security. Efforts to bring Iraq into compliance with UN Security Council resolutions requiring Saddam to dismantle Iraq's weapons of mass destruction programs had broken down, he said. With all alternatives to war having been exhausted, the use of force was therefore justified and necessary. No alternative conclusion was possible. Powell put his own personal reputation on the line. "Every statement I make today is backed up by sources, solid sources," he testified. "These are not assertions. What we're giving you are facts and conclusions based on solid intelligence."[33]

This turned out to be untrue. Upon examination, his characterization of the Iraqi threat proved to be misleading where not altogether fictitious. The intelligence reports forming the basis of those charges were concoctions built on half-truths and outright falsehoods. Its members unpersuaded, the Security Council withheld its assent. Ever the good soldier, Powell had done the bidding of his commander in chief. His personal reputation for veracity never recovered.[34]

The hawks in President Bush's inner circle did not regret Powell's failure; they welcomed it. The administration was now in a position to say: We asked; they refused; therefore, we have no choice but to do what needs doing. The self-conferred authority of the world's sole superpower more than sufficed to endow decisions made in the White House with an adequate legal and moral basis. As far as the Bush administration was concerned, the UN had rendered itself superfluous.

So, too, had Powell himself. Although the administration's organizational chart assigned him a place in Bush's inner circle, Cheney, Rumsfeld, and Wolfowitz disdained Powell. He lacked zeal. He did not share—and may not even have fully grasped—the immensity of the ambitions they entertained after 9/11. He was not one of their own. From their perspective, therefore, the blemishes now sullying Powell's previously untarnished reputation were not unwelcome. With America's first Black secretary of state discredited, no further obstacles impeded their path. And they were intent on going for broke.

In the wake of World War II, the first generation of wise men had positioned the United States to serve as primus inter pares. Their successors in the George W. Bush administration were intent on achieving something far grander: They wanted the United States to be simply and inarguably primus.

Bringing this new world order into existence wasn't expected to be all that difficult. The wise men took U.S. military supremacy as a given. That Iraqis, offered the chance, would welcome U.S. troops as liberators—such were Vice President Cheney's expectations—and willingly embrace American-style liberal democracy also figured as reasonable assumptions.[35] So six weeks after Powell's unsuccessful appearance before the Security Council, the wise men got the war that they so earnestly desired. Operation Iraqi Freedom—the name testifying to the illusions of the war's architects—commenced.

Disaster ensued. Indeed, the term "disaster" hardly suffices to describe the results of the Iraq War, with U.S. troops of all races paying a ghastly price.[36] Needless to say, none of the war's proponents lost their lives as a result of their bad judgment. With the passage of time, a surprising number of them found ways to rehabilitate themselves. White pundits who had gotten the war wrong showed an impressive aptitude for covering their tracks. Years later they were still appearing on the Sunday morning talk shows and pontificating on the editorial pages of the *New York Times* and the *Washington Post*.[37] Meanwhile, even as the United States was sustaining tens of thousands of casualties and expending trillions of dollars, it achieved few of its objectives.

As the war dragged on, Black Americans became less willing to enlist.[38] The All-Volunteer Force invited all potential recruits to formulate their own answer to *why we fight*. It came down to a matter of personal choice rather than obligation. On that score, the Iraq War prompted a larger number of potential Black enlistees to opt for no, thanks. Yet the war's racial dimension largely escaped notice—even when a Black man became commander in chief.

A Black Man Takes the Helm

With the Iraq War still very much under way, the presidential election of 2008 offered voters a clear choice. The Republican Party nominated Arizona senator John McCain. Embodying the elite tradition, McCain was committed to winning the ongoing war, whatever the cost. As their nominee, the Democrats chose Illinois senator Barack Obama, young, charismatic, whip smart, and Black.

Even before the Iraq War began, even before he had burst onto the national political stage, Obama had denounced the very idea of invading Iraq as "rash" and "dumb."[39] Implicit in his candidacy were expectations that as president he would not only end the war but would also chart a different course. Black in this context implied a willingness to reassess America's assumed position atop a post–Cold War global order. Black signified a willingness to question assumptions.

As far as that role in the world was concerned, the question hanging over the election was clear to all: Would Americans affirm claims to global leadership begun and nurtured over the course of decades? Or, in response to Iraq, would they renounce that project and embrace change? Ultimately, a clear majority cast their votes for change only to be rewarded with more of the same.

The nation's first Black president shied away from abandoning the project that traced its origins to the immediate aftermath of World War II. He signaled his intention through key appointments—retaining his predecessor's defense secretary and appointing as secretary of state a bellicose former senator who had voted in favor of invading Iraq. Robert Gates and Hillary Clinton were both unerringly loyal to the postwar/post–Cold War tradition of militarized American global leadership, as indeed was Joe Biden, Obama's choice for vice president.

The new commander in chief also wasted no time in affirming his own acquiescence to that tradition. During his first year in office, he tripled the number of U.S. troops in Afghanistan.[40] For years, the war there had languished in the shadows of Iraq; Obama now brought it to the fore. And although Obama kept President Bush's promise to withdraw from Iraq by December 2011, the end of the American combat mission there proved only temporary. In mid-2014, U.S. forces returned, embarking upon a new fight, this time against the Islamic State, an al-Qaeda offshoot. The new mission was another salvage operation. U.S. troops fought not to liberate, as in 2003, but to prop up a shaky regime installed at great cost following the overthrow of Saddam Hussein.

Critics of Obama's foreign policy quibbled and carped. Yet the wars begun after 9/11 continued. The president's actions made it clear that he was not backing away from the received definition of "what America is all about." Were there doubts on that score, his administration's participation in a brand-new campaign advertised under the heading of "liberation," this one focused on ousting Libyan dictator Muammar Gaddafi, squelched them. Hillary Clinton's jocular verdict on the outcome—"We came. We saw. He died."—was as revealing as it was crude. She omitted just a single phrase: "Because it serves our purposes that he should do so." Here, carried into the twenty-first century, was the standard elite rationale for employing force, dating from the first efforts to expel American Indians from land coveted by white settlers.[41] Under the nation's first Black president, that rationale remained intact.

In his second term, Obama did pursue several initiatives suggesting a desire to break free from the straitjacket of past policy. Among them were the 2016 Paris Climate Accord, a multilateral agreement to prevent Iran from acquiring nuclear weapons, and preliminary steps toward abandoning a decades-old policy of isolating Cuba. None of those efforts was destined, however, to outlast his administration.

What did outlive his presidency, almost unnoticed, was a comprehensive $1.7 trillion program to outfit the U.S. nuclear arsenal with new warheads, bombers, submarines, and missiles.[42] The architects of U.S. policy during the Cold War had persuaded themselves—and the American people—that the nation's security and survival depended on keeping a vast nuclear strike force at the ready. Obama was on record as favoring the abolition of nukes.[43] Instead, the preservation of nuclear overkill was to form a durable and lasting part of his legacy.

Today, elements of the military-industrial complex have turned to the task of designing and manufacturing B-21 Raider strategic bombers, Columbia-class missile-launching nuclear submarines, a new line of land-based intercontinental ballistic missiles, and a family of more flexible and "usable" warheads. Their labors keep alive the tradition of those who more than a half century ago designed and manufactured the H-Bomb, the B-52 Stratofortress, Polaris submarines, Minuteman ICBMs, and an arsenal ultimately consisting of more than thirty thousand nuclear weapons.[44]

By the time Obama left office, the Evil Empire of the Soviet Union had faded to a distant memory. Long wars and economic distress found the American "empire of liberty," to use Jefferson's phrase, looking battered and careworn. Yet the handiwork of the wise men—forces designed for global power projection, a sprawling network of bases abroad, very high levels of military spending and arms exports, and a penchant for armed intervention—remained fully intact. Over the course of his eight years in the White House, Obama failed to implement or even to articulate a credible alternative to the national security paradigm conceived in the immediate aftermath of World War II. He thereby acquiesced in its perpetuation.

No Longer Knowing Why We Fight

As the election of 2016 approached, a new phrase had entered the American political lexicon: "endless war." No doubt the term "endless" might strike some as over-the-top. As U.S. forces invaded, occupied, and attempted to transform various countries while punishing sundry regimes for their bad behavior, more accurate characterizations might have been "almost constant," superseded by "interminable," and culminating in "devoid of definable purpose."[45] At any rate, by 2016 a widespread impression that wars devoid of definable purpose and of interminable duration had become an almost constant part of American life played a not inconsequential role in determining the outcome of that year's presidential election.

That contest pitted Hillary Clinton, white, female, and the possessor of a matchless CV, against Donald Trump, also white and a male tycoon turned TV host with no apparent qualifications for high office.

Clinton was the candidate of the establishment, which was counting on her to maintain traditional national security policies. Trump was the candidate of the great unwashed, who by 2016 had lost confidence in that tradition and responded favorably to Trump's pledge "to keep us out of endless war."[46] To Trump's supporters, the national security elite had forfeited any right to be trusted. Their gripe had nothing to do with race, gender, or sexuality—all hot-button issues—but everything to do with competence: For all their fancy credentials, the twenty-first-century successors of Marshall, Acheson, and Lovett demonstrably lacked it.

The contest was Clinton's to lose. This she proceeded to do, in no small part because of her unwavering support for overseas adventurism. Clinton's defeat signified a rejection of all that the establishment stood for. It was as if in 1948 President Harry Truman had lost the White House to Henry Wallace, the former vice president whose accommodating attitude regarding the Soviet Union (and support from American Communists) horrified establishment hard-liners.

What Trump's victory actually signified in terms of an alternative approach to foreign policy was less clear. While the new president stood for America First, his unprincipled, erratic, and self-contradictory behavior in office made it difficult to discern the meaning of that phrase. On three points only did Trump demonstrate consistency. First was his determination to overturn anything that looked remotely like an Obama achievement. Second was his commitment to increasing military spending, regardless of whether any rationale existed for doing so. Third was his belief in his own personal ability to cut deals in direct talks with foreign leaders. On this score, China's President Xi Jinping, Russian president Vladimir Putin, and North Korean dictator Kim Jong-un demonstrated that Trump's smug self-confidence was badly misplaced.

Most significantly, however, Trump did not make good on his vow to end those endless wars. *Why we fight* languished as a question with no readily available answer.

The spring and summer of 2020 presented an opportunity to address that deficiency. As the coronavirus pandemic all but brought the nation to its knees, the economy tanked, and police killings of Black men and women provoked nationwide protests against racial injustice, Trump responded by washing his hands of all responsibility. He also overtly aligned himself with the cause of white nationalism. In doing so, the commander in chief forfeited what little remained of his moral authority.

With that, a moment unique in all of American history now presented itself: an opportunity for a distinctively Black viewpoint to serve as the basis for future U.S. global policy. As the first Black JCS chairman, Colin Powell had embraced a white definition of America's role in the world. Doing so had earned him plaudits from elites before destroying his reputation. As the first Black president, Barack Obama had shied away from abandoning outright the paradigm of militarized American global leadership. Doing so paved the way for Donald Trump to succeed him in the White House.

With the establishment discredited and Trump's efforts to devise an alternative approach to policy having produced nothing of value, the path to a new course of action informed by a heightened appreciation for the role of race in international affairs has presented itself. Call that approach Black-over-White.

Such an approach will no longer classify crimes committed by twentieth-century colonial empires (including the United States) as any less abominable than crimes committed by twentieth-century totalitarians. Rather than viewing events through the lens of great power competition centered on Eurasia, it will highlight the exploitation and deprivation of peoples inhabiting what political elites once disparaged as the Third World, where *third* implied "less important" and carried connotations of racial subordination. Rather than talking of peace to justify preparations for war, Black-over-White might well mean a serious commitment to equality, social justice, and genuine peace.

For now, the Black Lives Matter movement prioritizes other concerns, showing little inclination to reassess the handiwork of the wise men. Yet confronting domestic racism will inevitably require a critical examination of U.S. global policies tainted by racist assumptions, whether of recent vintage or from deeper in the past. Any movement genuinely committed to systemic social change will have to reassess and revise America's role in the world.

During World War II, Frank Capra's *Negro Soldier* incorporated Black Americans into a narrative casting that conflict as a crusade for freedom, deftly skirting past the fact that the war was also about maintaining racial hierarchies at home and abroad. Today, that bit of Hollywood fakery is no longer credible.

In twenty-first-century America, traditional hierarchies are collapsing. The impetus toward multiculturalism is irreversible. So, too, in all likelihood, are the demographic trends pointing toward the emergence of a majority minority population by the middle of the present century.[47] When that point arrives, the national security establishment is likely to find itself out of business.

Should the question *why we fight* once again command attention, as it inevitably will, Americans will not be satisfied with either the evasions of Frank Capra or the comforting nostrums of Colin Powell. Instead, the hard truths of Martin Luther King or even Eldridge Cleaver may prove more useful as sources of enlightenment.

7

KISSING YOUR EMPIRE GOODBYE

The handbook on "Effective Imperial Management" consists of three basic tenets. First: Don't invade Russia. Second: Share costs. Third: Repatriate benefits.

In the early nineteenth century, violating rule #1 cost Napoleon Bonaparte his crown as Emperor of the French and France its standing as the preeminent power on the Continent. In the twentieth century, Adolf Hitler made the identical mistake: His Thousand-Year Reich ended barely a decade after he announced its creation and less than four years after the Wehrmacht invaded the Soviet Union.

During the century when the sun never set on their empire, the British displayed a particular aptitude for tapping rule #2. As late as World War I, Canadians in astonishingly large numbers served on the Western Front, Anzacs in Gallipoli, Indians across the Middle East, and both Black and white South Africans in Africa, all at the behest of a King Emperor that few of them had ever laid their eyes on. Even the Irish served the Crown. In 1914, the Royal Irish Rifles, the Royal Inniskilling Fusiliers, and the Royal Irish Fusiliers formed part of the British Expeditionary Force that deployed to France and fought the initial engagements of the Great War.[1] Some might even argue that in 1917 and again after 1939, Britain's former North American colonies, having long since gained their independence, also came to the rescue of their former overlords.

Only after a second world war did the stores of loyalty among those imperial subjects dry up. And with that, the British Empire no longer remained a going concern.

As to purported benefits, some combination of reflected glory, booty, and the illusion of profitability may suffice to purchase compliance on the home front. But this works only as long as the going is good. Subjects need to believe that imperialism works for them. That describes the essence of rule #3. When the casualty lists are long, jobs scarce, and stomachs empty, singing "Deutschland, Deutschland über Alles!" or "Rule, Britannia!" loses its charm.

Disregard this canon of imperial management and you might as well kiss your empire goodbye. This describes the predicament faced by members of the U.S. national security elite as the Apocalypse of 2020 swept across the American Empire.

When the Going Was (Pretty) Good

In some quarters, the very existence of that empire remains a subject of dispute. Some but not all: Going back a century and more, critics have denounced "Yankee imperialism" in Mexico, throughout Central America and the Caribbean, and across the Pacific. During the 1960s, supporters of the Cuban Revolution and opponents of the Vietnam War cited American imperial-ism as the root of all evil. Since the end of the Cold War, few scholars specializing in U.S. policy abroad deny the existence of the American Empire, disagreeing only on its nature, contours, purpose, and prospects.

In the nation's capital, however, a well-entrenched habit of denial persists. There, politicians, diplomats, generals, and apologists of the establishment remain committed to the proposition that since the American Empire differs from the Roman and British precursors—the only two historical analogies deemed relevant—it doesn't qualify as an empire at all. American power is ostensibly sui generis. By extension, those who wield that power—accumulating arms, positioning forces abroad, and making decisions to bomb or invade or occupy—enjoy an exclusive prerogative to interpret what those actions signify.

President Joe Biden won't acknowledge the existence of an American Empire even as he labors to repair the damage that the empire sustained during his predecessor's term in office.

Yet the events culminating in the misfortunes of 2020 suggest that further denying the empire's existence will serve chiefly to accelerate its demise. Only by abandoning the pretense that the United States is immune to the temptations of empire will it be possible to avoid repeating the mistakes leading to the current crisis. The United States ignores the three rules of Effective Imperial Management at its peril.

During the heyday of our empire, from the end of World War II in 1945 to the U.S. invasion of Iraq in 2003, policymakers in Washington did a decent, if imperfect, job of adhering to those three rules.

Given the vastness of the Russian empire, then known formally as the Union of Soviet Socialist Republics, postwar

American strategists wisely suppressed any inclination to follow in the footsteps of Bonaparte or Hitler. The Soviet acquisition of nuclear weapons in 1949 eliminated any viable alternative to a strategy of containment. For the duration of the Cold War, rule #1 remained sacrosanct.

Implementing containment did require the stationing of U.S. troops abroad in unprecedented numbers and for an indefinite period. Especially in Western Europe, allies stepped up to share the burden. If NATO deserves its title as "the most successful alliance in history," it does so because from the 1950s through the 1980s member states recognized that upholding rule #2 was a matter of collective self-interest. Americans back home needed to know that the nation's junior partners were doing their fair share. Although this entailed finessing measures of actual fighting capability—European armies tended to underinvest in the wherewithal actually needed to wage war—America's NATO allies did contribute forces sufficient to invest a strategy of deterrence with credibility. As a result, Western Europe's de facto absorption into the postwar Pax Americana proved to be mutually agreeable.

As for rule #3, the unique economic circumstances existing in the aftermath of World War II spared Americans from confronting a guns versus butter trade-off. Maintaining the Pax Americana imposed some additional costs on the home front, with "peacetime" military expenditures far greater than in any earlier period of U.S. history. But those costs proved more than manageable. From the very outset of the Cold War, policymakers in Washington assumed that American industry could produce plenty of guns even as the American people enjoyed ample stocks of butter along with a cornucopia of consumer goods. That assumption proved correct.

According to NSC 68, a top secret document prepared in 1950 and destined to serve as a blueprint for postwar grand strategy, World War II proved that the American economy can "provide enormous resources for purposes other than civilian consumption while simultaneously providing a high standard of living."[2] The Cold War affirmed the compatibility of economic prosperity with an extended national security emergency. Not all shared equally in that high standard of living, of course, but enough did to persuade most Americans most of the time that the empire was mostly worth it.

The partial meltdown of the 1960s—assassinations, war, unrest, economic distress—did prompt some doubts about the Pax Americana's long-term prospects. In 1972, Senator George McGovern's "Come Home, America" presidential campaign put the question to a vote.[3] On Election Day, he won but a single state and a grand total of 17 electoral votes. While Americans wanted to be done with Vietnam, they were not ready to give up their empire.

Once the creation of the All-Volunteer Force freed the nation from further reliance on conscripts, both political parties took for granted the permanence of the American Imperium. Even after the fall of the Berlin Wall, the global posture prompted by the exigencies of the Cold War escaped serious attention. In 1992, the first presidential election after the fall of the Berlin Wall, the empire didn't even make it onto the ballot.

The opposing candidates, incumbent President George H. W. Bush and his challenger, Arkansas governor Bill Clinton, differed on many issues. But on one matter they were in lockstep: The uninterrupted exercise of American global leadership—the establishment's preferred euphemism for empire—qualified as a categorical imperative.

> Retreating from the world or discounting its dangers is
> wrong for our country and sets back everything we hope
> to accomplish. . . . The defense of freedom and a promo-
> tion of democracy around the world aren't merely a reflec-
> tion of our deepest values. They are vital to our national
> interest. . . . The stakes are high because the collapse of
> Communism is not an isolated event. It is part of a world-
> wide march toward democracy whose outcome will deter-
> mine the next century.[4]

The sentiments are Clinton's, but they could just as well
have come from Bush or any number of pundits, talking heads,
members of Congress, or presidential aspirants waiting in the
wings, all claiming the ability to decipher History's ultimate
purpose.

Three Amendments

As the nation's first baby boomer president, Bill Clinton viewed
himself as an agent of fundamental change, called upon to preside over the dawn of a new historical era. Not least among
his accomplishments was to formulate a distinctive approach
to Effective Imperial Management. Clinton did not explicitly
rescind the Three Rules that had prevailed during the Cold War.
Instead, he devised amendments suited to the circumstances created by its passing.

   If Clinton's approach to managing the empire had a theme,
it was captured in the old Johnny Mercer/Harold Arlen tune
"Ac-Cent-Tchu-Ate the Positive." Mercer's lyrics emphasized
the imperative of "Bring[ing] gloom down to the minimum"
and "spread[ing] joy up to the maximum." The ebullient and

opportunistic Clinton possessed a knack for doing both, as illustrated by his handling of two small wars that failed to follow their intended scripts.

In October 1993, during the first year of his presidency, insurgents in the Somali capital Mogadishu ambushed a contingent of U.S. Army rangers. In the ensuing firefight, eighteen American soldiers died, seventy-three were wounded, and one was taken captive. The sudden loss of elite troops caught the public completely by surprise. An intervention that had begun as a humanitarian relief mission had somehow morphed into bloody armed combat. President Clinton went on national TV to brief a shocked nation on what had occurred—or more accurately to obfuscate and deflect responsibility.

"In a sense," he explained, "we came to Somalia to rescue innocent people in a burning house. We've nearly put the fire out, but some smoldering embers remain."[5] In fact, the Clinton administration itself had recklessly poured gasoline on those embers. By attempting to impose on Somalis a political order of Western design, the United States (with UN backing) had fomented armed resistance to the presence of foreign troops. The Mogadishu street fight was a direct result.

Clinton's plans for his first term did not include a shooting war in an obscure country on the Horn of Africa. To prevent further losses, he charged U.S. diplomats with negotiating a tacit cease-fire with the insurgents, creating a decent interval during which U.S. forces could quietly withdraw. This departure occurred in March 1994, without the White House taking official notice. The last American officer to leave the scene told journalists, "I suggest you get out of here while you can."[6] Clinton himself had already moved on to other concerns. Thus did he "bring gloom down to a minimum."[7]

The Kosovo War of 1999, another intervention justified on humanitarian grounds, illustrates his ability to "spread joy up to the maximum." The purpose of Operation Allied Force was to end the brutalization of Kosovars by Serb forces operating at the behest of their leader Slobodan Milošević. The U.S. general in charge expected a campaign of three or four days' duration. Declining to play along, Serb ground forces demonstrated an annoying capacity to adapt and limit the effectiveness of U.S. and NATO airpower. Ultimately, it required seventy-eight days of ever-intensifying bombing, to include attacks in the heart of the Serb capital Belgrade, along with threats of a ground invasion, before Milošević gave in to allied demands.[8]

As Serb forces withdrew, the Kosovo Liberation Army immediately launched its own ethnic cleansing campaign aimed at ousting the quarter million Serbs and Roma then living in Kosovo.[9] Skirting past such unseemly details, Clinton portrayed the outcome as an unprecedented military and moral triumph—"a victory for a safer world, for our democratic values, and for a stronger America."[10] This was bunkum, but also vintage Clinton.

In the overall hierarchy of American battles, the embarrassment of Somalia compares to the siege of Fort McHenry near Baltimore in 1814, each immortalized by subsequent mythmaking. The defense of Fort McHenry inspired an anthem. Mogadishu inspired a best-selling book and a hit movie. As for the victory over the Serbs at Kosovo, we may liken it to the Battle of San Juan Hill in 1898. The subject of momentary acclaim, it was soon eclipsed by larger military developments and all but forgotten.

The experiences of Mogadishu and Kosovo (along with other

minor dustups involving the use of force) led Clinton to attach three de facto codicils to the prevailing rules of effective imperial management: 1) avoid using ground troops; 2) bank on airpower; and 3) declare success at the first possible moment and don't look back. In sum, bombs, not GI blood; symbolic action in lieu of decisive outcomes.

Clinton's three amendments, occasionally referred to as a "Clinton Doctrine," served him well politically. They enabled him to project an image of a tough-minded commander in chief while steering clear of anything approximating a Vietnam-style quagmire. As a basis for sound policy, however, those amendments were either irrelevant or illusory. Indeed, the wars initiated in the wake of 9/11 resulted in their peremptory repeal.

From the perspective of imperial management, Clinton's tenure as commander in chief was a lost opportunity. An administration less committed to accentuating the positive and eliminating the negative might have derived from Mogadishu and Kosovo important lessons. Differing from one another in setting and specifics, those two skirmishes offered complementary warnings. From Mogadishu: When facing off against irregulars in an urban setting, U.S. forces optimized for conventional combat fight at a severe disadvantage. From Kosovo: Even a technologically inferior adversary can pull tricks. To take such warnings seriously, however, was to call U.S. military supremacy into question, which during the 1990s neither the White House nor the Pentagon was willing to countenance.

Had the Clinton administration taken to heart the actual lessons of Mogadishu and Kosovo, the forces that invaded Afghanistan and Iraq after Clinton left office might have been better prepared for the surprises they were to encounter in both theaters. In that event, the American Empire might have been spared at least some of the damage it sustained during the ensuing era of "endless war."

Bill Clinton does not bear primary responsibility for all that went awry when war became endless. But neither is he altogether innocent. It was Clinton who allowed the United States to sleepwalk through the first decade of the post–Cold War era. Even as fresh threats to the American Empire were forming, he indulged in the fantasy of imperial impregnability.

When the Going Got Tough

The president who succeeded Bill Clinton had no patience with his predecessor's Three Amendments. "When I take action," George W. Bush told a handful of senators just days after 9/11, "I'm not going to fire a $2 million missile at a $10 empty tent and hit a camel in the butt. It's going to be decisive."[11]

With his reference to a missile in a camel's butt, President Bush was alluding to Clinton's penchant for pinprick air strikes. As commander in chief, Clinton had shown a pronounced aversion to risk. After 9/11, Bush was much worse: He was blind to risk. Using the empire itself as collateral, he was all about placing big bets. He rejected Clinton's Three Amendments and ignored the Three Rules.

Of course, Bush did not literally send troops into Russia. Yet his attempted "liberation" of Iraq (even as another campaign in Afghanistan was ongoing) served as the functional equivalent. In 1812, Napoleon Bonaparte counted on his seasoned and highly motivated Grande Armée and his own genius to overcome all obstacles. At the outset of Operation Barbarossa in 1941, Hitler's Wehrmacht was also a seasoned, highly motivated force, even if the Führer's generalship did not rise to Napoleonic levels. In each case, however, the invaders bit off far more than they could chew. Preliminary success led not to decisive victory but to a debilitating war of attrition.

A similar fate befell the U.S. troops that invaded Iraq in 2003. No one doubted the fighting power of American air, ground, and naval forces. And while American generalship might have fallen short of Napoleonic standards, it figured to be several notches above Adolf Hitler's. Still, the results were disastrous. Unlike the French and German legions that never made it to Moscow, U.S. troops did make it to Baghdad, only to discover that their accomplishment was strategically meaningless.

George W. Bush's Operation Iraqi Freedom equaled the folly of Bonaparte's and Hitler's attempts to conquer Russia, even if on a blessedly smaller scale. A common error links the three episodes: The quickest way to doom an empire is to expand when consolidation is the order of the day. Bonaparte in 1812 and Hitler in 1941 committed that cardinal imperial sin. So did Bush in 2003. None of those leaders recognized that his empire had reached its natural limits. None of them grasped the dangers of pressing further rather than firming up and consolidating what was already theirs.

According to rule #2, shrewd imperial managers find ways to off-load costs. In 1991, at the time of the Gulf War, George W. Bush's father offered a master class in how to do that. As the elder Bush's secretary of state, James Baker, put it, "We got other people to pay for the war." Administration efforts to persuade allies to cover the war's expenses, an enterprise jokingly referred to as Operation Tin Cup, defrayed an estimated 80 percent of the total cost of some $61 billion. Kuwait and Saudi Arabia, the immediate beneficiaries of Operation Desert Storm, each kicked in $16 billion. But Japan contributed $10 billion, Germany $6.4 billion, and the United Arab Emirates $4 billion.[12]

Their generosity derived not from charitable motives but from a conviction that even after the Cold War the Pax Americana still served their own purposes. Hence, their willingness to do their part in sustaining it by footing part of the bill.

The contrast with the post-9/11 wars is striking. No Tin Cup II materialized. Through the end of 2019, the cumulative costs of those conflicts exceeded $6.4 trillion, all of it put on the American taxpayer's credit card.[13] Neither Germany nor Japan, nor Saudi Arabia nor Kuwait, nor any other supposed beneficiary of the American Imperium volunteered to ease this country's burden. As a direct result, the national debt went through the roof. When the Bush administration embarked upon the Global War on Terrorism in 2001, the total national debt equaled $5.8 trillion. By the end of 2019, it had more than quadrupled, with annual increases in the trillions forecast for years to come.[14]

Of course, some in Washington argue that debt doesn't matter.[15] Prior to the Apocalypse of 2020 Americans could count on at least one political party going through the motions of calling for a balanced federal budget. Today the coronavirus pandemic has spurred the creation of a new bipartisan consensus: Fiscal responsibility is for wusses.

The managers of the American Empire have placed a large bet in assuming that no feasible alternative exists to the U.S. dollar as the world's reserve currency.[16] Yet even if this assumption holds true—and not everyone agrees that it will—the hemorrhaging of red ink is indicative of imperial mismanagement and misplaced priorities.[17] If nothing else, cumulative debt warps the allocation of resources. Today, for example, merely servicing the national debt costs the United States $600 billion per year, a sum roughly fifteen times larger than the amount appropriated annually to fund medical research by the National Institutes of Health.[18]

Would smaller debt service obligations have resulted in an NIH better prepared to respond to the coronavirus pandemic? We will never know. Even so, the disparity between the sum going to creditors and the sum going to public health speaks volumes about national priorities. During the decades that followed the Cold War, runaway costs did not deter the Congress from spending whatever it took to prop up the Pax Americana. Anticipating future dangers that might directly threaten the well-being of the American people figured as a lesser consideration.

As for rule #3, it became increasingly difficult after 9/11 to make the case that the American Empire was making life better for the average citizen. Critics on the far left and anti-interventionist right dared to suggest that the forever-wars version of global leadership might be a scam perpetrated by elites at the expense of ordinary citizens. Leading figures in Washington denounced that charge as vile slander, their rebuttal relying on vaporous rhetoric that steered clear of uncomfortable facts. Hard-pressed to demonstrate how the pursuit of global leadership was benefiting Joe or Joanie Six-Pack, they resorted to obfuscation. In short, they deceived.

As the Apocalypse of 2020 fell across the nation like some particularly loathsome smog, political deception became a major topic of conversation. President Donald Trump's penchant for misstatements, exaggerations, and bald-faced lies became a national scandal—and rightly so. Long prior to his arrival on the national political scene, however, ostensibly more reputable figures routinely perpetrated their own untruths about America's role in the world. This, too, amounted to lying, with implications as least as grave as Trump's idiotic prognostications about the coronavirus disappearing with the arrival of warm weather or his promotion of bogus cures.

Examples are legion, but here is one by a then serving secretary of state. "At the State Department," she said,

> we work in an international landscape defined by half a century of exceptional American global leadership, leadership from both parties, rooted in our most precious values, that put the common good first and rall[ied] the world around a vision of a more peaceful and prosperous future. Securing and sustaining that leadership for the next half century is the organizing principle behind everything I do. That's because our global leadership holds the key not only to our prosperity and security at home but to the kind of world that is increasingly interconnected and complex.

The previous half century to which Secretary of State Hillary Clinton was referring had included the Bay of Pigs and the Cuban Missile Crisis; the overthrow and assassination of South Vietnamese president Ngo Dinh Diem; secret bombing campaigns targeting Laos and Cambodia, countries with which the United States was not at war; tacit alliances with Mao Zedong's China and Saddam Hussein's Iraq among other unsavory regimes; and support for Afghan "freedom fighters" destined in time to launch a devastating terrorist attack against the American homeland. Bungled and costly wars in Afghanistan and Iraq followed in short order. None of these qualified for mention in Clinton's description of "exceptional American global leadership . . . rooted in our most precious values."

Secretary Clinton was perpetrating a fraud hardly less grotesque than any of Donald Trump's. Nor was she either the first or the last to engage in this deception. In her presentation at the Center for American Progress on October 12, 2011, Clinton was speaking in the reassuring patois of American Exceptionalism.[19] She was telling a group of Washington insiders precisely what they wanted and expected to hear. Not surprisingly, they responded to her presentation with warm applause.

Do attendees at events sponsored by that think tank or any of a dozen other comparable Washington institutions genuinely believe such sentiments? Did Soviet apparatchiks during the latter years of the Cold War genuinely believe the tripe about the wonders of Marxism-Leninism peddled by party leaders? Or does sustaining the pretense of belief serve other purposes, such as preserving privilege or safeguarding the status quo? Such questions are not easily answered.

This much is certain, however: In Washington, refusal to abide by the expected rhetorical conventions of American global leadership offers sufficient grounds for being effectively silenced. Critics of empire like Noam Chomsky on the left and Patrick Buchanan on the right offer examples. Each may be allowed his say and each may even attract large audiences. But in this instance, audience does not translate into influence. To question American Exceptionalism and oppose the American Empire is to become persona non grata wherever members of the foreign policy establishment congregate. That describes Chomsky and Buchanan's fate.

It also helps explain the establishment's antipathy toward Donald Trump both as a candidate and as president. On matters related to foreign policy, he appeared to delight in violating the protocols of exceptionalism. Whatever his faults, he was an emperor who dared to charge that the empire itself had no clothes.

A self-described master of the deal, Trump lambasted the American Empire as a bad bargain that found the American people paying through the nose and getting little in return. As to what should replace U.S. global leadership as an organizing principle of policy, he had nothing to offer. Trump was a heretic who rejected received dogma while proposing to substitute in its place the where's-my-cut ethics of New York City's real-estate scene. He was a Martin Luther intent on shaking down a Catholic Church awash with corruption in order to snag a share of Rome's ill-gotten gains.

Trump was the foreign policy establishment's worst nightmare. Yet his idiosyncratic version of anti-imperialism resonated with ordinary Americans who were losing their taste for empire. By 2020, for people worried about becoming sick, losing their jobs, or falling victim to seemingly indelible racism, "exceptional American global leadership" ostensibly "rooted in our most precious values" had become disconnected from their everyday concerns.

The onset of the Apocalypse offered a made-to-order chance to inventory the damage sustained through decades of reckless imperial mismanagement. The foreign policy establishment was, of course, disinclined to pursue that opportunity. Intent on preventing the empire's dissolution by continuing to deny its very existence, foreign policy elites as ever privileged their own interests over the nation's. That the American people would thereby pay an increasingly heavy price was all but certain.

8

THE HISTORY THAT MATTERS

"History is now and England," poet T. S. Eliot wrote in 1942.[1] Not anymore. For Americans today, history is us and it's fluid. The past necessarily centers on our story, but that story is in transition.

Prior to 2020, at least, the history deemed to matter in the estimation of most Americans emphasized the period from 1914 to 1989, with the United States occupying the center of the global stage, for much of that time in solitary splendor.

In former defense secretary Donald Rumsfeld's famous taxonomy of *known knowns*, *known unknowns*, and *unknown unknowns*, the History That Matters (HTM) occupies its own special niche.[2] That niche consists of *mythic knowns*—things widely accepted as true that ought to be taken with a grain of salt.

Chief among the mythic knowns to which most Americans have reflexively subscribed are these: that history has an identifiable shape, direction, and destination; that it is purposeful, tending toward the universal embrace of values indistinguishable

from American values; that pursuant to propagating those values, history confers on the United States unique responsibilities
and prerogatives.

By no means purporting to include every jot and tittle of
the entire American story, the HTM reduced the past to its pith
or essence. Like the Ten Commandments, it identified specific
shalts and shalt nots. Like the Sermon on the Mount, it pre-
scribed a code of behavior. In doing so, it made the past usable.
Endlessly reiterated in political speeches and reinforced by popular culture, the "lessons" of this usable past stipulated what
the United States was called upon to do and what it needed to
refrain from doing.

This usable past found expression in a straightforward narrative casting the twentieth century as the First American Century,
shaped throughout by the actions (or inaction) of the United
States. Although incorporating setbacks and disappointments,
the narrative culminated in reassuring triumph. Americans could
take satisfaction in the knowledge that, on balance, things were
headed in the right direction.

The drama unfolded in three acts, each centered on a large-
scale military undertaking.

The first, World War I, occurred between 1914 and 1918.
When that conflict began, Americans were having none of it.
Yet after considerable hesitation, urged on by a president who
believed it incumbent upon the New World to save the Old, they
took the plunge. The United States went off to fight, Woodrow
Wilson declared, "for the ultimate peace of the world and for the
liberation of its peoples," a stirring vision considerably at odds
with the actual war aims of the belligerents on both sides.[3]

Alas, the war brought neither permanent peace nor liberation.

No sooner did it end than Americans began having second thoughts. Revisionist historians like Harry Elmer Barnes, eventually joined by Charles A. Beard—among historians of his day an acknowledged superstar—argued that U.S. entry into the Great War had been a huge blunder.[4] Ever so briefly, scholarship reflected and reinforced the mood of the moment. When that moment passed, however, revisionism fell out of fashion and the approved version of history resumed its onward march. Rather than an unmitigated disaster, World War I and its aftermath came to represent a missed opportunity. It seemingly warned of the consequences that result when the United States falters in its obligation to lead.

Act II began in 1939 or 1938 or 1936 or 1933—the date dependent on the "lesson" to which you're calling attention—but ended definitively in 1945. World War II offered Americans a second chance to grasp the baton of global leadership.[5] The war pitted good against evil, freedom against slavery, civilization against barbarism, and democracy against dictatorship.

Not merely in myth but also in fact, World War II was all of those things. But it was much more as well. It was a winner-take-all contest between rival claimants to Pacific dominion, between competing conceptions of how to govern peoples regarded as inferior, and between two decidedly different brands of totalitarianism, one of them, the Soviet version, aligned (for the moment) with the United States. One thing World War II was emphatically not: a war to avert genocide. During the war itself, the fate of European Jews facing extermination at the hands of Nazi Germany attracted mere passing attention and became a *raison de guerre* only as an afterthought.

Per Donald Rumsfeld, we might categorize such realities as

discomfiting knowns. Crediting Europe's liberation to the Anglo-American alliance—forged by Franklin and Winston singing "Onward Christian Soldiers" aboard HMS *Prince of Wales*—makes for a suitably uplifting tale.[6] Acknowledging the Red Army's far larger contribution to defeating the Nazi menace—with Eastern Europeans subsequently paying a steep price for their "liberation" at Soviet hands—only serves to complicate things. The preferred American version of the past has a decided aversion to complications.

Lasting considerably longer than the first two acts combined, Act III ran from roughly 1947 to 1989 and consisted of many scenes, some of which resisted easy incorporation into the HTM: nuclear arsenals bristling with thousands of weapons, partnerships with unsavory despots, coups and assassination plots by the bushel, not to mention Korea, the Bay of Pigs, the Cuban Missile Crisis, and Vietnam, capped off when the Leader of the Free World, aka Richard Nixon, exchanged pleasantries in Beijing with Red China's murderous Great Helmsman, Mao Zedong. All of this made it difficult to cast Act III as a virtuous sequel to Act II.

Historians took note. A new generation of revisionists, the disciples of William Appleman Williams prominent among them, challenged the official line depicting the Cold War as another round of good pitted against evil, freedom against slavery, civilization against barbarism, and democracy against dictatorship.[7] They dared to suggest that imperial ambitions permeated the American project. Among proponents of historical orthodoxy, those revisionists provoked outrage.[8] At least briefly, the past seemed once more up for grabs. For a time, a debate among American historians engaged broad public attention.

The end of the Cold War deflected that challenge. Instead,

the version of the past to which Americans had become accustomed emerged clothed in triumphal regalia. To wide applause, a political scientist announced that history itself had ended.[9] Snicker if you will, but when Francis Fukuyama's article "The End of History?" appeared in the summer 1989 issue of the *National Interest*, it received a reception akin to that of a verdict handed down from on high. "The triumph of the West, of the Western *idea*," Fukuyama wrote, "is evident first of all in the total exhaustion of viable systematic alternatives to Western liberalism." History's trajectory and purpose now appeared self-evident, as did America's extraordinary singularity.

In 1992, an unproven presidential candidate reduced the History That Matters to a homely parable. "I am literally a child of the Cold War," Bill Clinton began.

> My parents' generation wanted little more than to return from a world war and resume the blessedly ordinary joys of home and family and work. Yet . . . history would not let them rest. Overnight, an expansionist Soviet Union summoned them into a new struggle. Fortunately, America had farsighted and courageous leaders . . . who roused our battle-weary nation to the challenge. Under their leadership, we helped Europe and Japan rebuild their economies, organized a great military coalition of free nations, and defended our democratic principles against yet another totalitarian threat.[10]

In declaring his fealty to this narrative, Clinton was seeking to establish his credibility as a would-be statesman, by saying precisely what his listeners were expecting of him. He was affirming what all of them had learned in grammar school and heard at patriotic celebrations, a chronology reinforced and even sanctified by countless movies and TV shows. If Clinton had concluded his presentation with a promise of "liberty and justice for all," his purpose could not have been more transparently obvious. Yet this was more than mere political posturing. Implicit in Clinton's succinct and reassuring account of the past was a template applicable to policy challenges to come.

Of course, history had not ended. When new challenges duly appeared, Clinton's successor reflexively reverted to that familiar template. For President George W. Bush, the need for yet another large-scale military enterprise comparable to those that had made the twentieth century an American Century was self-evident. The History That Matters all but demanded it—especially if you were seeking to be a President Who Mattered.

The ensuing Global War on Terrorism, in effect, constituted a continuation of history's onward march. To highlight the continuities, some observers styled the U.S. response to 9/11 as "World War IV," with the Cold War retroactively designated World War III.[11]

Alas, by whatever name, World War IV proved to be a bust. While the endeavor began with assurances of decisive victory, decision proved to be illusive. Indeed, before World War IV had entered its second decade, no plausible conception of how exactly the United States might achieve victory was to be found. Muddling through had become the order of the day.

Revisionism with a Vengeance

In 2016, a real estate tycoon turned celebrity denounced the standard narrative of the past and won the White House. Donald Trump's credentials as a student of history were thin at best.

But in seizing upon "America First" as a central theme of his candidacy, Trump gleefully upended historical orthodoxy.

Decades before, America Firsters had been consigned to a place in history roughly on a par with the Tories who had opposed independence in 1776. In some precincts (to include my alma mater, West Point), Confederate generals who in the course of attempting to destroy the Union had killed thousands of American soldiers still retained places of honor. Not those who prior to Pearl Harbor had opposed coming to the aid of Great Britain in its war against Nazi Germany. Purveyors of orthodoxy regarded the actions of these America Firsters as indefensible and their cause beyond the pale.

Among the myriad outrages perpetrated by President Trump, his efforts to redeem America First are unlikely to rank as his worst. But they may prove to have been among the most subversive. Over the course of U.S. history, American Exceptionalism had incorporated two themes. According to the first, America was to serve as an exemplar. According to the second, America was to liberate. Whether consciously or intuitively, Trump was now proposing to substitute a third theme: American Exceptionalism as a grant of privilege, providing that in any "deal" Americans should get more than their fair share. No more having their pockets picked. No more indulging free riders. No more getting played for suckers by conniving foreigners. This was American Exceptionalism stripped of any moral content.

Trump thereby kicked open the door to a kind of historical revisionism that in short order dwarfed anything undertaken by the likes of Harry Elmer Barnes, Charles Beard, and William Appleman Williams. Trump's undisguised disdain for conventional moral standards offended the guardians of American Exceptionalism in either of its traditional forms. As an unintended by-product, it empowered anyone daring to question the moral basis of the American experiment.

Revisionists debunk. They break china. In attitude, they tend toward insolence. Twentieth-century revisionism had emanated from the slightly disreputable fringes of American intellectual life, both right and left. The principal sponsor of the new revisionism, making its appearance just prior to the spasms of 2020, was the *New York Times*, the most influential publication in the nation, if not the world. Without firing a shot, revisionists thereby captured a primary citadel of the establishment.

This twenty-first-century revisionism had a quintessentially Trumpian quality. It was nothing if not brash. Rather than merely taking aim at the American Century, it rewrote the narrative of the American Founding. For the new revisionists, the trials and tribulations that the United States had overcome on its journey to global ascendency no longer defined the history that really mattered. Instead, the relevant past began in 1619, when the first African slaves arrived in colonial Virginia.[12] Everything that had ensued since stemmed from that fateful moment.

"No aspect of the country that would be formed here has been untouched by the years of slavery that followed," according to the newspaper's 1619 Project, and by the institutionalized racism that followed the abolition of formal slavery. The explicit purpose of this endeavor was to "reframe" the history of the United States "by placing the consequences of slavery and the contributions of black Americans at the very center of our national narrative."

If only implicitly, the 1619 Project responded to the tiki torch–wielding white racists and neo-Nazis who paraded through Charlottesville, Virginia, in August 2017 chanting, "You will not replace us!"[13] Perhaps not replace, the *New York Times* replied, but consider yourselves hereby demoted to a lower rank in the hierarchy of Americanness.

Even more boldly, the project questioned the very foundation of the nation's political legitimacy. The enterprise formally known as the United States of America derives its legitimacy from the Revolution of 1776, supposedly justified by self-evident truths and ostensibly undertaken in pursuit of inalienable rights, central among them a commitment to liberty. Nikole Hannah-Jones, director of the 1619 Project, now dismissed this as balderdash, asserting that "one of the primary reasons the colonists decided to declare their independence from Britain was because they wanted to protect the institution of slavery." In short, the purpose of the American Revolution was not to secure freedom but to deny it.

The aim was to create not only a new historical narrative, but a new historical consciousness. This was revisionism on a breathtaking scale.

To the guild of academic historians, the 1619 Project was a slap in the face, further evidence of that guild's declining status. In fact, more was at stake than mere turf. But the unrest sweeping American cities during 2020 seemed to validate the project's premises. Here, propelled from the bottom up and disclosed in real time, was a radically different take on the History That Matters.

Toppling the Statues

Whatever the product—a song, a movie, a new line of deodorant, an idea—timing is everything. Whether reflecting the genius of its architects or sheer dumb luck, the 1619 Project benefited from impeccable timing.

As President Trump was deriding the old historical ortho-doxy, here was the *New York Times* offering an up-to-the-minute replacement. By the spring and summer of 2020, race had once more claimed a place at the forefront of American politics. Mul-tiple episodes of police brutality, most prominently the killing of George Floyd on May 25 in Minneapolis, drove a stake through the Obama-era fantasy of an emerging post-racial society. Sym-biotically connected to Black Lives Matter, the 1619 Project offered a plausible and, for many citizens, a compelling histor-ical context in which to understand those disturbing events.

An extraordinary reckoning with America's past provided a context for interpreting the eruptions of 2020. To judge by the tidal wave of media commentary denouncing racism (accompa-nied by an abundance of virtue signaling), the history to which most Americans—make that white Americans—professed alle-giance now turned out to have actually consisted of an unbro-ken saga of abuse and brutality. Atonement, therefore, became the order of the day.

So down came the statues honoring Confederate generals and soldiers, not to mention once revered figures like Christopher Columbus and Junipero Serra. Institutions large and small went to very public lengths to expunge past connections with slav-ery and racism. In New York City, the leaders of the American Museum of Natural History ordered the removal of an eques-trian statue of Theodore Roosevelt due to its "hierarchical com-position," the offending statue depicting TR astride a horse with an American Indian and an African American walking alongside.[14] The NFL franchise long known as the Washington Redskins became the Washington Football Team. At Princeton University, the Wilson School, honoring a former president of the university and of the United States, became the Princeton School of Public and International Affairs, Woodrow Wilson's undisputed racism negating every other aspect of his career.

To some observers, this urge to purge recalled the Stalinist show trials of the 1930s, Maoist coerced self-criticism, or, closer to home, the postwar Red-baiting of the House Un-American Activities Committee and Senator Joseph McCarthy.[15] Predictably (and admirably), members of the American intelligentsia hastened to the barricades to decry these efforts to impose intellectual conformity.[16]

But defining the matter at hand as a dispute between free thought and politically correct thought overlooked an altogether different and arguably more substantive dimension. To redefine the past in light of a convergence between the 1619 Project and the Black Lives Matter movement was necessarily to embark upon a wholesale refashioning of America's role in the world.

The old narrative that prevailed until the train wreck of the Trump presidency had faced outward. It privileged the exercise of American global leadership abroad over all other concerns. Running the world defined the nation's first priority. While not totally oblivious to injustice and inequality at home, the HTM rated these as lesser priorities.

Sustaining these arrangements was a conception of American Exceptionalism not merely as an assertion of virtue but as a call to arms. America was not merely to be but to do. The experience of the United States in World War II and the outcome of the Cold War seemed to ratify its unique historical calling.

Whether American Exceptionalism in any form will survive the Apocalypse of 2020 ranks as an open question. After all, the 1619 Project, amplified by the megaphone of the *New York*

Times, asserts that the American experiment was conceived in iniquity. View the past through that lens and racism displaces liberty as the unifying theme of U.S. history.

So the fresh take on the History That Matters now forming could well prompt an inward turn. The imperative will be for America to transform itself into something other than what it has been—and certainly what it had become in the so-called Age of Trump.

In vowing to oust Donald Trump from the White House, Joe Biden acknowledged—and perhaps validated—this shift in priorities. Early in his run for the presidency, Biden was still reciting clichés, promising to restore the nation to its accustomed place as acknowledged leader of the global order. By August 2020, in accepting the nomination of the Democratic Party, he had embraced a revised version of the History That Matters. Rather than promising to save the world, he now presented himself as an agent of *domestic* renewal. Indeed, his explicit vow to save "the soul of the nation" hinted at his own version of an America First agenda even as he steered clear of that radioactive phrase.[17]

Of course, the traditional narrative that had prevailed in policy circles after 9/11 and throughout the years marked by the Global War on Terrorism, the presidency of Donald Trump, and the coronavirus pandemic (among other shipwrecks) took it as a given that saving both the world and America's soul were perfectly compatible. By Election Day in November 2020, that proposition appeared increasingly untenable.

Between 1989, when history supposedly ended, and 2020, when Americans were encountering more history than they could comfortably digest, the nation had endured a plethora of unwelcome surprises. During that short interval, history resumed with a vengeance, signaling its return by laying various ambushes into which Americans blindly stumbled. By whatever measure—lives lost or ruined, businesses destroyed, trust in basic institutions eviscerated—the resulting costs proved to be enormous.

That comparable surprises may lie just ahead seems likely. If once rid of Trump, political elites resurrect the comforting nostrums of the familiar HTM, they will all but guarantee such surprises. And should the accumulation and projection of military power, justified by claims of American Exceptionalism, once more define the central theme of American statecraft, then more needless wars, more waste, and more neglect of pressing priorities at home will result. And probably more Trumps as well.

FACTS, NOT FEELINGS

In May 2002, the *New Republic* published a lengthy essay by Leon Wieseltier, the magazine's longtime literary editor. "Hitler Is Dead," the title announced.[1] A Jewish American, Wieseltier directed his essay to his fellow Jews. Gentiles might reflect on his ruminations, but they were not the author's intended audience.

Wieseltier's message, delivered in a learned and eloquent wrapping, was this: Get a grip. Jews in Israel and in the United States, in his view, were losing touch with reality. "The community is sunk in excitability, in the imagination of disaster," he wrote. "There is a loss of intellectual control. Death is at every Jewish door. Fear is wild. Reason is derailed. Anxiety is the supreme proof of authenticity. Imprecise and inflammatory analogies abound."

The proximate causes of this anxiety were terrorist attacks within Israel orchestrated by Hamas and a U.S administration that Wieseltier characterized as "leaderless and inconstant." As a result, feverish worries that a Second Holocaust was imminent fed on one another. Citing dire predictions of various American Jews and non-Jews who were anticipating the worst and soon, Wieseltier quoted the writer Nat Hentoff: "If a loudspeaker goes off and a voice says, 'All Jews gather in Times Square,' it could never surprise me."

Wieseltier dismissed this "Jewish panic" as "purely recreational," serving chiefly as an excuse to avoid sober analysis. That anti-Semitism persisted was undeniable. So did threats to Israeli security. Equally undeniable, Wieseltier noted, was the fact that a nuclear-armed Israel was considerably stronger than any of its regional adversaries. As for the Jews who lived in America, they were "the spoiled brats of Jewish history" and "the luckiest Jews who ever lived."

"The Jewish genius for worry has served the Jews well," Wieseltier acknowledged, "but Hitler is dead." By implication, to treat the genuine evil that Hitler had represented as a harbinger of things to come was to transmute reasoned wariness into outright paranoia. While such self-indulgence might provide a frisson of manufactured trepidation, it was unlikely to provide an accurate gauge of reality.

"The facts, the facts, the facts," Wieseltier counseled, "and then the feelings." To allow feelings to take precedence over facts was to put actual security at risk.

Spoiled Brats

If ever a people deserved recognition as history's spoiled brats, it is the privileged tribe known as Americans, especially members of the generation fortunate enough to have been born at the dawn of the American Century. In 2002, when Leon Wieseltier chastised his fellow Jews for allowing fears to take precedence over facts, he ought to have directed his reproof to a much wider audience.[2] It was Wieseltier's fellow Americans, Jewish or not, who needed that reminder.

After all, in 2002, the United States was gearing up to invade Iraq. According to those making the case for war, Saddam Hussein represented a mortal threat, with the elimination of his regime an urgent moral and strategic imperative.[3] Here was a classic case of fears, sparked by 9/11 but compounded by rashness, riding roughshod over facts. Yet the ensuing Iraq War was by no means the first instance during the American Century when this had occurred.

For Jews (whether American or not) and for Americans (whether Jewish or not), this tendency to privilege fears over facts stemmed in large part from the period 1939–1945, or more specifically from the meaning assigned to the reign of terror perpetrated by Nazi Germany. For both groups (and most especially for Jews who are also Americans), the primary lesson of World War II was unambiguous and irrefutable: This must never happen again.

For Jews, *never again* refers to the Holocaust and (for many) to the requirement to maintain in Eretz Israel an indestructible sanctuary for the entire Jewish people. For Americans, especially for those who are not Jewish, *never again* warns against the United States ever shirking its responsibilities. Whereas the war against the Nazis threatened Jews with extermination, it delivered America to the apex of global power. For Israeli governments, *never again* establishes survival as the ne plus ultra of statecraft. For the U.S. government, *never again* is a call to action.

Soon after World War II, this summons formed the basis for a durable foreign policy consensus. As a conscious expression of historical learning, that consensus centered on avoiding any recurrence of the mistakes made during the 1930s in belatedly and ineffectually responding to the gathering danger posed by Hitler. The United States would permanently forswear isolationism. It would maintain at the ready mighty armed forces. It would never appease. It would come to the aid of those victimized by aggression. It would resist evil.

During the Cold War, adherence to the canonical lessons of World War II paved the way for various costly decisions, prominent among them the 1950 intervention in Korea and the full-scale Americanization of the Vietnam War in 1965. Presidents Harry Truman and Lyndon Johnson both cited the supposed lessons of World War II in justifying their actions.[4]

Even so, finding solace in its familiarity, the "never again" school's most devout adherents remained firmly moored to its terms. Thus did the Joint Comprehensive Plan of Action of 2015, better known as the Iran nuclear deal, elicit innumerable comparisons of Iran to Nazi Germany and Barack Obama to British prime minister and arch-appeaser Neville Chamberlain.[5] By the second decade of the twenty-first century, Marx's famous axiom about history repeating itself first as tragedy and then as farce was playing out in real time.

Casting Off the Muck

The Apocalypse of 2020 is itself a call to collective action. But it should also serve as a summons to reflect on the consequences of allowing fears—or self-gratifying conceits—to take precedence over facts. Hitler is indeed dead and gone, as is the terror he perpetrated. By extension, so, too, are the circumstances that gave rise to the American Century, which today is also dead and gone, if still awaiting a decent burial.

The challenges now facing Americans—assuming they remain committed to the aspirations specified in the Preamble of the Constitution—are of an entirely new order. This book identifies the most salient of those challenges, which run the gamut from economic, technological, and military to geopolitical, historical, and intellectual. Some, like the enduring legacy of American racism, are specific to the United States. Others, such as pandemics or climate change, operate on a planetary scale.

The cumulative crises of 2020 simultaneously illuminated and diverted attention from those challenges. As the death toll from COVID-19 mounted and unemployment soared, members of a besieged public grasped that things were going off the rails. Yet such public angst left the two main political parties remarkably unmoved.

The uncontested Republican nomination of Donald Trump to a second term affirmed the moral bankruptcy of the GOP. And while innovative proposals like the Green New Deal enabled impatient progressives to grab headlines, the Democratic Party's choice of a career politician to challenge Trump tacitly affirmed that centrists remained firmly in control. Joe Biden was a safe choice, but he was no one's idea of an inspiring one. One could be grateful for his eventual victory in the November 2020 election without finding any particular reason to celebrate.

A country in virtual free fall was invited to choose between an incumbent who had done nothing to forestall disaster and an aging warhorse given to rambling and verbal gaffes.

Of France in 1940, Marc Bloch wrote, "The men who govern us today were . . . brought up in mental bogs." The judgment applies in spades to the American political establishment of 2020.

Navigating an escape from those bogs will not come easily. Much like the French General Staff that waited passively while the Wehrmacht prepared to attack, the dominant factions in both political parties and the most influential voices in the commentariat remain imprisoned by an obsolete mental framework. Still, identifying principles that just might move the United States in a more positive direction remains possible.

The first order of business must be to establish priorities. For the foreseeable future, leading the world will have to take a back seat to repairing the nation. The French Army's assumption in 1940 that the next war would be just like the last one paved the way for failure. American leaders shackled to the assumption that the global distribution of power created by the end of the Cold War in 1989 will exist forever and a day invite a comparable outcome. Repairing itself at home will require the United States to acknowledge that its brief turn as sole superpower has not only ended but that its passing finds the country facing difficulties that in 1989 were unimaginable.

Unless the American people consent to a prolonged run of multitrillion-dollar deficits, repairing America will dictate a change in fiscal priorities. The share of discretionary spending allotted to the military-industrial complex will have to shrink considerably, while neglected domestic priorities related to matters such as economic equality, racial justice, health care, and infrastructure will require increased funding.

To prioritize domestic needs does not mean turning away from the world. It does mean addressing the world mindful of facts rather than fears or illusions.

Toward Responsible Statecraft

As an alternative to a failed strategy of militarized hegemony, the United States should move toward a posture of *sustainable self-sufficiency*. As a basis of strategy, sustainable self-sufficiency will maximize U.S. freedom of action. It will acknowledge the changing nature and distribution of global power. And it will take into account the lurking prospect of environmental cataclysm.

In the aftermath of the American Apocalypse, tweaking and tinkering won't do. What's required is a wholesale transformation of national security policy on a scale not seen since the outbreak of the Cold War. If there is defunding to be done, it should begin not with the police but with the Pentagon.

A strategy of sustainable self-sufficiency prioritizes real and immediate threats over distant and hypothetical ones. It focuses on things that directly endanger the well-being of the American people. It posits that proximity, whether temporal or geographic, correlates with importance.

What should this mean in practice? First, it means clearing away deadfall and cutting back overgrown shrubbery. Several too-long-taken-for-granted extracontinental security commitments offer examples.

Dating from the founding of the North Atlantic Treaty Organization more than seventy years ago, U.S. security guarantees to Europe have today become redundant. French president Emmanuel Macron himself has called for the creation of a "sovereign Europe" that "guarantees every aspect of [European] security."[6] A strategy of sustainable self-sufficiency will welcome this prospect, with the aim of nudging a free, democratic, and prosperous Europe to defend itself. The United States should, therefore, announce its intention to withdraw from NATO within the next decade. After a decent interval, United States European Command (EUCOM) should declare "mission accomplished," case its colors, and depart.

Can anyone doubt that the Global War on Terrorism, initiated by George W. Bush twenty years ago, has failed?[7] The GWOT was a misguided proposition from the very outset. As countless observers, including U.S. military commanders, have conceded, there is no military solution to terrorism.[8] What linger today in places where U.S. troops remain—Afghanistan, Iraq, and Syria, for example—are operations devoid of any larger strategic rationale.

Acknowledging this manifest failure, policies that prioritize sustainable self-sufficiency will liquidate the U.S. military presence in the Greater Middle East. United States Central Command (CENTCOM) and United States Africa Command (AFRICOM) should close up shop. The United States will once more classify terrorism as a criminal matter, falling under the purview of courts and law enforcement agencies, local, national, and international, rather than armies. U.S. policy in the Greater Middle East should henceforth de-emphasize military presence in favor of diplomatic engagement, working to solve problems rather than exacerbating them.

The case of East Asia differs: Under a strategy of sustainable self-sufficiency, the United States should continue to maintain a military presence there. Here, once more, the axiom "First, do no harm" applies.

The rise of China and provocations by the Chinese government have caused unease throughout the region. A potential new Cold War centered on Asia looms. The possibility of an actual shooting war cannot be excluded. An abrupt change in the U.S. military posture in the Indo-Pacific could trigger such a disaster. An emphasis on sustainable self-sufficiency will help to avert such a prospect.

The United States and China are rivals. Yet as American and Soviet leaders demonstrated during the Cold War when capping the nuclear arms race, rivalry need not preclude cooperation. Shared concerns on matters related to climate, commerce, and technology can potentially provide the basis for a Sino-American relationship that may not be warm but need not be overtly hostile. For now, however, United States Indo-Pacific Command will avoid the fate of EUCOM, AFRICOM, and CENTCOM.

More fundamentally, however, the approach to basic policy that I am recommending should pay greater attention to cultivating our own vast and rich but neglected garden. That garden is North America, encompassing Canada, Mexico, and the United States, an area of 9.54 million square miles that is home to 579 million people. Since World War II, U.S. policymakers preoccupied with Europe and the Far East, and subsequently with the Persian Gulf, took continental security more or less as a given—an oversight for which the United States paid dearly on 9/11.

A strategy of sustainable self-sufficiency, therefore, would entail an explicit reordering of priorities. It will reassert the obvious: What happens in North America is of far greater relevance to the well-being of the American people than anything that occurs in Europe, the Middle East, Africa, or East Asia. In the hierarchy of U.S. bilateral relationships, Canada and Mexico should come first.

Threats to Canadian territorial sovereignty as the Arctic melts, for example, matter more to the United States than any danger Russia may pose to Ukraine.[9] The Mexican government's inability to secure its borders and deal with drug cartels poses a greater danger to Americans than does Saudi Arabia's rivalry with Iran or Israel's difficulties with Hamas or Hezbollah.[10]

Therefore, in place of the military architecture left over from the Cold War, a strategy of sustainable self-sufficiency should center on ensuring the inviolability of a new North American Security Zone (NASZ). Rather than serving as an instrument of global power projection, the U.S. military should make common cause with Canadian and Mexican forces in maintaining the integrity of the NASZ perimeter, safeguarding the maritime, aerial, and cyber approaches to the continent.

This narrower remit will allow for a reallocation of resources earmarked for security. A military establishment charged with doing less will be able to get by with less. Cutting the Pentagon's budget will free up money for those agencies charged with providing immediate day-to-day protection to the American people. Examples include the Centers for Disease Control and Prevention, the Drug Enforcement Administration, the Environmental Protection Agency, the Federal Emergency Management Agency, Immigration and Customs Enforcement, the National Institutes of Health, and the U.S. Coast Guard. Each of these plays an essential and underappreciated role in enabling Americans to flourish and enjoy freedom where they live.

Bolstering these agencies will create within the NASZ a de facto defense in depth. In 2020, however, the cumulative budget of all these agencies came to a mere $91.4 billion, only 12 percent of the amount appropriated for the army, navy, air force, and Marine Corps.[11] A strategy of sustainable self-sufficiency will amend that disparity.

Sustainable self-sufficiency is not a euphemism for isolationism. The government of the United States can and should encourage global trade, investment, travel, scientific collaboration, educational exchanges, and sound environmental practices. Even with a more modest overseas U.S. military profile, all of these can continue.

Meanwhile, pivoting away from militarized globalism makes it possible to address other underattended needs. Self-sufficiency implies energy independence, which is both essential and achievable given sufficient attention to developing renewable sources. Responding to the wake-up call of the coronavirus pandemic, an emphasis on sustainable self-sufficiency will ensure that the United States retains within its borders the ability to manufacture the wherewithal required to address any health emergency on any scale.[12] Other requirements should include the ability of government at all levels to anticipate and respond to climate-exacerbated natural disasters, both at home and throughout the NASZ. For political elites keen for the United States to lead, here is a great opportunity: America can lead the world in demonstrating the benefits of genuine preparedness.

A strategy of sustainable self-sufficiency means shrinking the navy in favor of a larger and more capable coast guard.[13] It means terminating plans to field a costly arsenal of new planet-destroying nuclear weapons in favor of expanding the production of planet-friendly renewable energy. Instead of spending billions of dollars to develop a next-generation strategic bomber—estimated cost $550 million per aircraft—it means modernizing and expanding the aging air fleet the Forest Service relies on to fight fires of ever-increasing scope and intensity.[14] Rather than relentlessly pursuing a way of life based on consumption and waste, it means taking seriously a collective obligation to bequeath a livable planet to future generations. It means embracing some version of the proposed Green New Deal.

Here then is the ultimate payoff: A strategy of sustainable self-sufficiency just might enable a government accustomed to squandering lives and dollars to become a government that nurtures and preserves.

Almighty Superpower No More

Almost everyone has a favorite artifact—a trinket, memento, or souvenir. Mine is a tattered copy of the *New York Times Magazine*, dated March 28, 1999. Filling the cover is an oversize and vividly painted photograph of a clenched fist. Red and white stripes cover wrist and palm. The fingers are a deep blue, with a pattern of evenly spaced white stars. It is Old Glory repurposed as a symbol of incomparable power.

The fist belongs to a white male—pale skin peeks from the cuticle of the thumbnail. In 1999, white males were long accustomed to wielding power and the *Times Magazine* accommodated that tradition. For anyone unable to interpret the photo, an accompanying text deciphered its meaning: "For globalism to work, America can't be afraid to act like the almighty superpower that it is."

"Almighty superpower"! Pause here to consider that this emphatic claim appeared a mere twenty years before the *Times* magazine launched its 1619 Project, rendering the United States not as an almighty superpower but as an undertaking born in a state of sin. Eons rather than decades separate the two moments.

In 1999, the triumphalism of the early post–Cold War era still lingered, not least of all in the pages of the *Times*. In fact, that era was already on its last legs. Were there any doubts on that score, the sundry disasters and close calls of 2020 should now have removed them. To pretend otherwise serves no purpose. To escape from our era of ideological fantasy requires taking stock of the dismal consequences that American arrogance and misjudgment have yielded since we thought the world was ours.

The facts, the facts, the facts, and then the feelings, with no room for illusions. Then, perhaps, we can save our country.

NOTES

A NOTE TO THE READER

1. For a concise profile, see Mike Dash, "History Heroes: Marc Bloch," *Smithsonian Magazine* (November 10, 2011).
2. The quotations are from Marc Bloch, *Strange Defeat: A Statement of Evidence Written in 1940* (New York: W. W. Norton [reprint], 1968).

INTRODUCTION

1. Art Cullen, "Drought, Plague, Fire: The Apocalypse Feels Nigh," *Guardian* (September 15, 2020).
2. Sasha Abramsky, "The Climate Apocalypse Has Arrived," *Nation* (August 25, 2020).
3. Damon Linker, "Living Through the Apocalypse," *Week* (September 18, 2020).
4. Annie Wiener, "An Apocalyptic August in California," *New Yorker* (August 24, 2020).
5. Maya Weldon-Lagrimas, "Apocalypse in California—Coming to You Soon," *Yale Daily News* (September 11, 2020).
6. For a devasting summary of those failures, see Joel Achenbach, William Wan, Karin Brulliard, and Chelsea Janes, "The Crisis That

Shocked the World: America's Response to the Coronavirus," *Washington Post* (July 20, 2020).

7. William D. Hartung and Mandy Smithberger, "Boondoggle, Inc.: Making Sense of the $1.25 Trillion National Security State Budget," *TomDispatch* (May 7, 2019).

8. Andrew J. Bacevich, *American Empire: The Realities and Consequences of U.S. Diplomacy* (Cambridge, MA: Harvard University Press, 2002). For the full text of Albright's interview, see the online State Department archive at https://1997–2001.state.gov/statements/1998/980219a.html, accessed April 6, 2020.

9. World Islamic Front, "Jihad Against Jews and Crusaders" (February 23, 1998), https://fas.org/irp/world/para/docs/980223-fatwa.htm, accessed April 6, 2020. This document charged, among other things, that "for over seven years the United States has been occupying the lands of Islam in the holiest of places, the Arabian Peninsula, plundering its riches, dictating to its rulers, humiliating its people, terrorizing its neighbors, and turning its bases in the Peninsula into a spearhead through which to fight the neighboring Muslim peoples."

1: OLD, NEW, NEXT

1. "A Time of Great Uncertainty: An Interview with Pope Francis," *Commonweal* (April 8, 2020).

2. As an example, see Glenn Kessler, Salvador Rizzo, and Meg Kelly, "President Trump Made 16,241 False or Misleading Claims in His First Three Years," *Washington Post* (January 20, 2020).

3. Joseph R. Biden Jr., "Why America Must Lead Again," *Foreign Affairs* (March/April 2020).

4. Katie Glueck and Thomas Kaplan, "Joe Biden's Vote for War," *New York Times* (January 12, 2020).

5. Arthur M. Schlesinger Jr., *The Crisis of the Old Order* (Boston: Houghton Mifflin, 1957), 49, 50, 54, 75.

6. "America's Changing Religious Landscape," Pew Research Center on Religion and Public Life (May 12, 2015).

7. "Biden Says He Told Foreign Leaders 'America Is Back,'" *CBS News* (November 11, 2020).

8. "Looking to the Future, Public Sees an America in Decline on Many

Fronts," Pew Research Center on Social and Demographic Trends (March 21, 2019).

9. Schlesinger, *Crisis of the Old Order*, 485.

10. "The heat, generally speaking, kills this kind of virus," he told a meeting of state governors at the White House in mid-February 2020. "A lot of people think that goes away in April as the heat comes in. We're in great shape though, we have 12 cases, 11 cases, but we're in very good shape." Andrew Buncombe, "Coronavirus Outbreak: Trump Cautioned for Insisting Deadly Virus 'Will Be Gone by April,'" *Independent* (February 10, 2020).

11. John Adams, Letter to Thomas Jefferson (February 2, 1816).

12. George Orwell, *As I Please, 1943–1945* (Boston: Harcourt, Brace & World, 1968), 166.

13. This is the definition of militarism that I use in my book *The New American Militarism: How Americans Are Seduced by War* (New York: Oxford University Press, 2005), 2.

14. "The Secretary of State to the Ambassador in the United Kingdom (Kennedy)," *Foreign Relations of the United States, Diplomatic Papers 1939; General*, vol. 1, 542. The State Department sent identical notes to Berlin, Paris, Rome, and Warsaw.

15. "Bombing, States and Peoples in Western Europe 1940–1945," Centre for the Study of War, State and Society, University of Exeter [UK] (n.d.).

16. "Bombing of Tokyo," *Encyclopaedia Britannica* (last updated March 2, 2020); "Hiroshima and Nagasaki Death Toll," *Children of the Atomic Bomb*, http://www.aasc.ucla.edu/cab/200708230009.html, accessed April 10, 2020.

17. "Bombing of North Korea," Wikipedia, https://en.wikipedia .org/wiki/Bombing_of_North_Korea#cite_note-ROK_Web-31, accessed April 10, 2020.

18. Charles Hirschman, Samuel Preston, and Vu Manh Loi, "Vietnamese Casualties During the American War: A New Estimate," *Population and Development Review* (December 1995).

19. Alden Whitman, "Reinhold Niebuhr Is Dead; Protestant Theologian, 78," *New York Times* (June 2, 1971).

20. Reinhold Niebuhr, *The Irony of American History* (New York: Scribner, 1952), 79.

21. In 1966, Niebuhr charged that "we are making South Vietnam into

an American colony by transmuting a civil war into one in which Americans fight Asians while China, the presumed enemy, risks not a single life." "Reinhold Niebuhr Discusses the War in Vietnam," *New Republic* (January 29, 1966).

22. Niebuhr, *Irony of American History*, 174.
23. Quoted in Whitman, "Reinhold Niebuhr Is Dead," Niebuhr's *New York Times* obituary.

2: THE ECLIPSE OF THE WEST

1. James Monroe, "Annual Message to Congress" (December 2, 1823).
2. William H. McNeill, "What We Mean by the West," *Orbis* (Fall 1997), 520.
3. Winston Churchill, "Sinews of Peace [Iron Curtain Speech]," Westminster College, Fulton, Missouri (March 5, 1946).
4. Samuel P. Huntington, "The Clash of Civilizations?," *Foreign Affairs* (Summer 1993).
5. For a sample, see the essays collected in *The Clash of Civilizations? The Debate* (New York: Foreign Affairs, 1996).
6. Bill Clinton, "Address to a Joint Session of Congress" (February 17, 1993).
7. For further elaboration on this point, see Andrew J. Bacevich, *The New American Militarism: How Americans Are Seduced by War* (New York: Oxford University Press, 2005).
8. Robert Kagan, "Power and Weakness," *Policy Review* (June/July 2002).
9. Gulf War air campaign, https://en.wikipedia.org/wiki/Gulf_War_air_campaign; Opération Daguet, https://en.wikipedia.org/wiki/Op%C3%A9ration_Daguet#Operations_%E2%80%93_air_and_naval_phase, accessed April 22, 2020.
10. John E. Peters et al., *European Contributions to Operation Allied Force* (Santa Monica, CA: RAND, 2001), Table 2–1.
11. "NATO Bombing of Yugoslavia," https://en.wikipedia.org/wiki/NATO_bombing_of_Yugoslavia; "1999—Operation Allied Force," https://www.afhistory.af.mil/FAQs/Fact-Sheets/Article/458957/operation-allied-force/, accessed April 20, 2020.
12. "Blair's War," *Frontline* documentary for PBS, produced by Dai Richards. The quoted official was Benoît D'Aboville.

13. George W. Bush, "State of the Union Address" (January 29, 2002).

14. Tony Blair to George Bush, "Note on Iraq," [July 2002], https://www.theguardian.com/uk-news/2016/jul/06/with-you-whatever-tony-blair-letters-george-w-bush-chilcot#img-1, accessed April 24, 2020.

15. "Blair Is Bush's Poodle, George Michael Sings," *Toronto Globe & Mail* (July 2, 2002).

16. "Statement by France to Security Council," *New York Times* (February 4, 2003).

17. John Hooper, "German Leader Says No to Iraq War," *Guardian* (August 6, 2002).

18. Jonah Goldberg, "Frogs in Our Midst," *National Review* (July 16, 2002). Goldberg did not coin the phrase but proudly claimed credit for being its "most successful populizer."

19. John Hooper and Ian Black, "Anger at Rumsfeld Attack on 'Old Europe,'" *Guardian* (January 24, 2003).

20. James Naughtie, "How Tony Blair Came to Be So Unpopular," *BBC News* (July 9, 2016).

21. Stephan A. Carney, *Allied Participation in Operation Iraqi Freedom* (Washington, DC: U.S. Army Center of Military History, 2011).

22. "Private Security Contractors in Iraq: Background, Legal Status, and Other Issues," *Congressional Research Service* (September 29, 2009).

23. For illustrative purposes, see the ISAF "placemat" from February 2009, https://www.nato.int/isaf/placemats_archive/2009–02–13-ISAF-Placemat.pdf, accessed April 29, 2020.

24. Donald Rumsfeld, "Text: Rumsfeld's Pentagon News Conference," *Washington Post*, October 18, 2001.

25. Stephen M. Saideman and David P. Auerswald, "Comparing Caveats: Understanding the Sources of National Restrictions upon NATO's Mission in Afghanistan," *International Studies Quarterly* (March 2012).

26. More formally known as the UKUSA Agreement, Five Eyes provides a mechanism for sharing in the collection and analysis of highly classified intelligence traffic.

27. Biden for President website, https://joebiden.com/, accessed May 1, 2020.

28. Philip Sim, "Scottish Independence: Could a New Referendum Still Be Held?" *BBC News* (January 31, 2020).

29. Andrew Chatzky and James McBride, "China's Massive Belt and Road Initiative," *Council on Foreign Relations Backgrounder* (January 28, 2020).

30. "Remarks by President Trump to the 72nd Session of the United Nations General Assembly" (September 19, 2017).

31. Andrew Beaton, "A Million N95 Masks Are Coming from China—on Board the New England Patriots' Plane," *Wall Street Journal* (April 2, 2020).

32. George H. W. Bush, "A Europe Whole and Free" (May 31, 1989). This was a speech delivered by President Bush in Mainz, Germany.

3: NOT SO SPECIAL

1. George Washington, "Farewell Address to the Nation" (1796).

2. Michael H. Hunt, *The Making of a Special Relationship: The United States and China to 1914* (New York: Columbia University Press, 1983), 24–25, 170–72.

3. Arthur Henderson Smith, *Chinese Characteristics* (Shanghai: Shanghai North China Herald, 1890), 387. Italics in the original.

4. Arthur Henderson Smith, *The Uplift of China* (New York: Church Missionary Society, 1908), xv, 48.

5. "Pearl Buck's Speech at the Nobel Banquet at the City Hall in Stockholm" (December 10, 1938).

6. "Christmas Eve Speech—Report on the Tehran Conference" (December 24, 1943).

7. Zach Fredman, "The Longer History of Imperial Incidents on the Yangtze," *Modern American History* 3, no. 1 (2020): 87–91. For more on this theme, see also Fredman's *From Allied Friend to Mortal Enemy: The U.S. Military in Wartime China* (Chapel Hill: University of North Carolina Press, forthcoming). For an excellent fictional rendering of relations between ordinary Chinese and American sailors in China between the world wars, see Richard McKenna, *The Sand Pebbles* (New York: Harper & Row, 1962).

8. "Remarks Delivered by Vice President Mike Pence on the Administration's Policy Towards China at Hudson Institute" (October 4, 2018).

9. Quoted in Yaacov Bar-Simon-Tov, "The United States and Israel Since 1948: A 'Special Relationship'?" *Diplomatic History* (April 1998), 231.

10. "Britain's Forgotten War," *BBC News* (April 20, 2001), http://news .bbc.co.uk/2/hi/uk_news/1285708.stm, accessed May 26, 2020.

11. Ministry of Defence, "UK Armed Forces Quarterly Service Personnel Statistics" (February 2020), https://assets.publishing.service .gov.uk/government/uploads/system/uploads/attachment_data/file /866842/1_Jan_2020_-_SPS.pdf, accessed May 26, 2020.

12. Alex Winston, "Israel Drops a Slot in 2019 Military Strength Ranking, Still Behind Iran," *Jerusalem Post* (August 12, 2019). Total active duty strength of the IDF is 170,000 with another 445,000 reserves.

13. For a brief description of the intelligence-sharing partnership, which includes, along with the United States and the United Kingdom, Australia, Canada, and New Zealand, see Office of the Director of National Intelligence, "Five Eyes Intelligence Oversight and Review Council (FIORC)" (undated), https://www.dni.gov/index.php/ncsc -how-we-work/217-about/organization/icig-pages/2660-icig-fiorc.

14. They were *The Gathering Storm* (2002, with Albert Finney as Churchill); *Into the Storm* (2009, Brendan Gleeson); *Darkest Hour* (2017, Gary Oldman); *Churchill* (2017, Brian Cox); and on PBS *Churchill's Secret* (2016, Michael Gambon). During that same period, Hollywood all but ignored Churchill's American contemporaries, producing no biopics about President Franklin Roosevelt or Harry Truman and just one about Dwight D. Eisenhower. *Ike: Countdown to D-Day* (2004), featuring Tom Selleck as Eisenhower, left the American historical consciousness undented.

15. Rachel Weiner, "Winston Churchill Bust Back in Oval Office," *Washington Post* (January 20, 2017).

16. Jen Chaney, "Why *Downton Abbey* Became a Massive Cultural Phenomenon," *Vulture* (March 6, 2016), https://www.vulture.com /2016/03/downton-abbey-why-it-mattered.html, accessed June 9, 2020.

17. Lucy Baugher, "'Downton Abbey' Exhibition to Go on Tour in the U.S.," *Telly Visions* (October 14, 2017), https://blogs.weta.org /tellyvisions/2017/10/14/downton-abbey-exhibition-go-tour-us, accessed June 9, 2020.

18. For one notably assertive example, see candidate Donald Trump's speech to the American Israel Public Affairs Committee (AIPAC) on March 21, 2016, https://www.cnn.com/videos/politics/2016/03 /21/donald-trump-aipac-bts-tsr.cnn, accessed June 9, 2020.

19. Michael B. Oren, *Ally: My Journey Across the American-Israeli Divide* (New York, 2015), 376.

20. "Concerned About Nuclear Weapons Potential, John F. Kennedy Pushed for Inspection of Israel Nuclear Facilities," National Security Archive (April 21, 2016), https://nsarchive.gwu.edu/briefing -book/nuclear-vault/2016–04–21/concerned-about-nuclear -weapons-potential-john-f-kennedy, accessed June 9, 2020.

21. For a detailed summary of that controversy, see "USS Liberty Incident," https://wikispooks.com/wiki/USS_Liberty_Incident, accessed June 9, 2020. For a perspective that absolves Israel of any malign intent, see Michael Oren, "The USS Liberty: Case Closed," *Azure* (Spring 2000).

22. David K. Shipler, "Israeli Jets Destroy Iraqi Atomic Reactor; Attack Condemned by U.S. and Arab Nations," *New York Times* (June 9, 1981).

23. Matthew Bell, "Jonathan Pollard, American Traitor and Israeli Hero, Will Go Free," *World* (July 29, 2015).

24. "Iron Dome," https://en.wikipedia.org/wiki/Iron_Dome#:~:text =The%20bill%20provides%20%24235%20million,system%20 in%20the%20United%20States, accessed June 17, 2020.

25. The term refers to the small-scale, recurring use of force to degrade enemy capabilities in protracted conflicts where no resolution appears possible. Efraim Inbar and Eitan Shamir, "Mowing the Grass in Gaza," *Jerusalem Post* (July 22, 2014).

26. Unable to pay cash, Israel negotiated a loan from the United States at 3.5 percent interest, repayable over ten years. Hayim Iserovich, "Hawks vs. Doves: The Story of the First US-Israel Arms Deal," *IsraelDefense* (August 8, 2018).

27. David Tal, "Symbol, Not Substance? Israel's Campaign to Acquire Hawk Missiles, 1960–1962," *International History Review* (June 2000), 304–17.

28. "U.S. Foreign Aid to Israel," *Congressional Research Service* (updated August 7, 2019), https://www.everycrsreport.com/reports/RL33222 .html#Content, accessed June 19, 2020.

29. "Israel-United States Relations," https://en.wikipedia.org/wiki /Israel%E2%80%93United_States_relations#:~:text=More%20 recently%2C%20in%20fiscal%20year,also%20received%20sig nificant%20economic%20assis, accessed June 18, 2020.

30. "Funded by US, Now Israel's Iron Dome Maker Expects to Sell It Back," *Middle East Eye* (September 27, 2018).

31. Jason Sherman, "US Army Scraps $1b. Iron Dome Project, After Israel Refuses to Provide Key Codes," *Times of Israel* (March 7, 2020).

32. Michael Crowley and David M. Halbfinger, "Trump Releases Mideast Peace Plan That Strongly Favors Israel," *New York Times* (February 4, 2020).

33. Martin Indyk, "The Middle East Isn't Worth It Anymore," *Wall Street Journal* (January 17, 2020).

4: STRANGE DEFEATS, AMERICAN-STYLE

1. *The U.S. Army in the Iraq War* (2 vols.) (Carlisle Barracks, PA: Army War College Publications, 2019). The title page of each volume lists six different editors and contributors. Volume 1 consists of 739 pages, including notes, maps, illustrations, and bibliography. Volume 2 adds another 713 pages.

2. *The U.S. Army in the Iraq War*, vol. 2, 615, 616.

3. A notable exception to this dearth of attention was "The Last War— and the Next?," a thoughtful review essay by Jon Finer in the July/ August 2019 issue of *Foreign Affairs*.

4. "Joint Vision 2020," *Joint Forces Quarterly* (Summer 2000).

5. Jacob Heilbrunn, "The Rumsfeld Doctrine," *New York Times Book Review* (April 30, 2006).

6. For a concise rendering of the rise and fall of "shock and awe," see John T. Correll, "What Happened to Shock and Awe?," *Air Force Magazine* (November 1, 2003).

7. For an example of premature journalistic cheerleading, see Tom Bowman, "U.S. Demonstrates 'New Style' of Warfare in Iraq," *Baltimore Sun* (April 13, 2003).

8. For a reminder of the consequences when bombing operations went wrong, see Tom Engelhardt, "Washington's Wedding Album from Hell," *TomDispatch* (December 20, 2013).

9. Available data is at "U.S. Air Forces Central," https://www.afcent.af .mil/About/Airpower-Summaries/, accessed September 28, 2020. For additional statistics, see https://www.wired.com/2012/01/afghan -air-war/#more-65463 and https://www.wired.com/images_blogs

/dangerroom/2010/12/30-November-2010-Airpower-Stats.pdf, also accessed on September 28, 2020.

10. On April 3, 2003, an Iraqi Roland surface-to-air missile downed an Air Force A-10 close air support aircraft. The pilot survived and was recovered.

11. Neta Crawford, "Human Cost of the Post-9/11 Wars: Lethality and the Need for Transparency," Costs of War Project, Brown University (November 2018).

12. Dan Murphy and Gordon Lubold, "US Commander in Iraq: I Need More Soldiers, More Time," *Christian Science Monitor* (March 9, 2007).

13. *The U.S. Army in the Iraq War*, vol. 2, 616.

14. General Daniel H. Berger, "Force Design 2030" (March 2020).

15. David Lartner and Aaron Mehta, "With DoD's Fleet of 2045, the US Military's Chief Signals He's All-In on Sea Power," *Defense News* (October 6, 2020).

16. "The Army's Vision and Strategy," n.d., https://www.army.mil/about/, accessed October 23, 2020.

5: NATURE BITES BACK

1. "Bunker Hill I (CV-17)," Naval History and Heritage Command, https://www.history.navy.mil/research/histories/ship-histories/danfs/b/bunker-hill-i.html, accessed May 3, 2020.

2. "USS Theodore Roosevelt, CVN 71," http://www.uscarriers.net/cvn71history.htm, accessed May 4, 2020.

3. "USS Theodore Roosevelt COVID-19 Cases Exceed 1,100, Navy to Decrease Reporting," [San Diego] *City News Service* (May 1, 2020).

4. A video of the send-off is at https://www.nbcnews.com/news/us-news/videos-show-sailors-cheering-navy-captain-relieved-command-after-raising-n1175946, accessed May 4, 2020.

5. Matthias Gafni and Joe Garofoli, "Exclusive: Captain of Aircraft Carrier with Growing Coronavirus Outbreak Pleads for Help from Navy," *San Francisco Chronicle* (March 31, 2020).

6. William A. Buckingham Jr., *Operation Ranch Hand: The Air Force and Herbicides in Southeast Asia, 1961–1971* (Washington, DC: Office of Air Force History, United States Air Force, 1982), 10. This is the official U.S. Air Force history of the defoliation campaign. The officer quoted was Lieutenant General Lionel C. McGarr, U.S. Army.

7. All Kennedy administration NSAMs, with supporting documentation, are at https://www.jfklibrary.org/archives/other-resources/national-security-action-memoranda-nsams.

8. Murrow's dissent is contained in National Security Action Memorandum 178, Subject: "Destruction of Mangrove Swamps in South Vietnam," dated August 16, 1962.

9. Buckingham, *Air Force and Herbicides in Southeast Asia*, 199–201.

10. "Agent Orange" (May 16, 2019), https://www.history.com/topics/vietnam-war/agent-orange-1, accessed May 6, 2020.

11. For details, see Andrew J. Bacevich, *America's War for the Greater Middle East: A Military History* (New York: Penguin Random House, 2016), chap. 2.

12. For a book-length account of the U.S. military's recovery from Vietnam, see James Kitfield, *Prodigal Soldiers: How the Generation of Officers Born of Vietnam Revolutionized the American Style of War* (New York: Simon & Schuster, 1995).

13. "Congressional Testimony of Dr. James Hansen, June 23, 1988," https://www.sealevel.info/1988_Hansen_Senate_Testimony.html, accessed May 7, 2020.

14. John Noble Wilford, "His Bold Statement Transforms the Debate on Greenhouse Effect," *New York Times* (August 23, 1988).

15. *National Military Strategy of the United States* (January 1992), 7.

16. *National Military Strategy of the United States of America: A Strategy of Flexible and Selective Engagement* (1995), 3.

17. "National Security Implications of Climate-Related Risks and a Changing Climate" (July 23, 2015).

18. *National Military Strategy: Shape, Respond, Prepare Now* (1997).

19. *The National Military Strategy of the United States of America: A Strategy for Today; A Vision for Tomorrow* (2004), 23.

20. *The National Military Strategy of the United States of America: The United States Military's Contribution to National Security* (June 2015), 4.

21. "Gerald R Ford Class—US Navy CVN 21 Future Carrier Programme" (n.d.), https://www.naval-technology.com/projects/cvn-21/, accessed May 17, 2020.

22. For a detailed discussion, see Alexandra Homolar, "Rebels Without a Conscience: The Evolution of the Rogue States Narrative in US Security Policy," *European Journal of International Relations* (December 2011), 705–27.

23. Thomas B. Cochran et al., *Nuclear Weapons Data Book*, vol. 1, *U.S. Nuclear Forces and Capabilities* (Cambridge, MA: Ballinger Publishing Company, 1984), 15, Table 1-6. The U.S. stockpile of nuclear weapons peaked at a total of 32,500.

24. Katie Benner and Adam Goldman, "F.B.I. Finds Links Between Pensacola Gunman and Al Qaeda," *New York Times* (May 18, 2020).

25. William D. Hartung and Mandy Smithberger, "America's Defense Budget Is Bigger Than You Think," *Nation* (May 7, 2019).

26. Michael Schwirtz, "The 1,000-Bed Comfort Was Supposed to Aid New York. It Has 20 Patients," *New York Times* (April 2, 2020).

27. "When to Watch the Blue Angels Fly over Chicago, Detroit and Indianapolis Today" (May 12, 2020), https://www.cnn.com/2020/05/12/us/blue-angels-chicago-detroit-indianapolis-fly-over-trnd/index.html, accessed May 20, 2020.

28. The literature is voluminous, but for a small sample, see John Schwartz, "Humans Are Making Hurricanes Worse. Here's How," *New York Times* (September 19, 2018).

29. For a primer, see Robert Richardson, "Depleting Earth's Resources," MSU Today (August 1, 2018), https://msutoday.msu.edu/news/2018/depleting-earths-resources/, accessed May 20, 2020.

30. Elizabeth Kolbert, "The Sixth Extinction?," *New Yorker* (May 18, 2009); Ariella Simke, "There Is Plastic in Your Fish," *Forbes* (January 21, 2020).

31. "Increased Drought Severity Tracks Warming in the United States' Largest River Basin," *PNAS: Proceedings of the National Academy of Sciences of the United States of America* (May 11, 2020).

32. Kaiser Family Foundation, "The HIV/AIDS Epidemic in the United States: The Basics" (March 25, 2019).

33. Centers for Disease Control and Prevention, "Climate Effects on Health" (May 14, 2020), https://www.cdc.gov/climateandhealth/effects/default.htm, accessed May 21, 2020.

34. "List of Natural Disasters in the United States," https://en.wikipedia.org/wiki/List_of_natural_disasters_in_the_United_States, accessed May 21, 2020.

35. Alistair Gee and Dani Anguiano, "We Created the Anthropocene and the Anthropocene Is Biting Back," *Guardian* (May 5, 2020).

6: WHY WE FOUGHT/WHY WE FIGHT

1. Frank Capra, *The Name Above the Title: An Autobiography* (New York: Citadel, 1971), 325–43.
2. The narrator of *Why We Fight* was the distinguished American actor Walter Huston.
3. *Why We Fight: Prelude to War*, https://www.youtube.com/watch?v=pX64RgQbqOg. The entire series is available online.
4. The entire Civil War receives seventeen seconds of mention, consisting of quotes from Abraham Lincoln with the Lincoln Memorial as a backdrop. The entire film is available online at https://www.youtube.com/watch?v=dln2dQyLNVU. The U.S. Navy produced its own, less artful equivalent called *The Negro Sailor*, also online at https://www.youtube.com/watch?v=ji1aG5s9qI4.
5. For an image of the poster, available from Walmart, see https://www.walmart.com/ip/The-Negro-Soldier-movie-POSTER-Style-A-11-x-17–1944/115890043, accessed June 20, 2020.
6. In recognition of their generous support of the Pentagon (and despite their attitudes regarding race), for example, the U.S. Navy named one aircraft carrier (CVN70) after Representative Carl Vinson of Georgia and another (CVN74) after Senator John Stennis of Mississippi, along with a nuclear attack submarine (SSN687) after Senator Richard Russell of Georgia. None of the three qualified even remotely as an advocate of civil rights.
7. For a discussion of the CPUSA's position on race, see Timothy Johnson, "'Death for Negro Lynching!' The Communist Party, USA's Position on the African American Question," *American Communist History* (no. 2, 2008).
8. Jennifer Wilson, "When the Harlem Renaissance Went to Communist Moscow," *New York Times* (August 21, 1971).
9. "Special Message to the Congress Reporting on the Situation in Korea" (July 19, 1950).
10. Morris J. McGregor, *Integration of the Armed Forces, 1940–1965* (Washington, DC, Center of Military History, United States Army, 2001), chap. 17.
11. The first anti-lynching bill was introduced in 1918. Only in 2020 did the Emmett Till Antilynching Act become law. For details, see

https://www.congress.gov/bill/116th-congress/house-bill/35/text, accessed June 22, 2020.

12. There were no African American general officers on active duty with the U.S. Army in 1965. In 1968, Colonel Frederic E. Davidson, who was Black, was promoted to brigadier general.

13. Gerald F. Goodwin, "Black and White in Vietnam," *New York Times* (July 18, 2017).

14. In an address delivered at the Johns Hopkins University in April 1965, President Lyndon Johnson offered his administration's justification for the Vietnam War. For the text of this important speech, see http://www.lbjlibrary.org/exhibits/the-presidents-address-at-johns -hopkins-university-peace-without-conquest, accessed July 6, 2020.

15. Bob Orkand, "I Ain't Got No Quarrel with Them Vietcong," *New York Times* (June 27, 2017).

16. Martin Luther King, "Beyond Vietnam—A Time to Break Silence" (April 4, 1967).

17. "To My Black Brothers in Vietnam," *The Black Panther* (March 21, 1970).

18. For a concise narrative, see David Cortwright, "Black GI Resistance During the Vietnam War," *Vietnam Generation* (1990), https://digitalcommons.lasalle.edu/cgi/viewcontent.cgi?article =1052&context=vietnamgeneration#:~:text=The%20stron gest%20and%20most%20militant,with%20greater%20deter mination%20and%20anger, accessed June 25, 2020.

19. For a vivid contemporary account, see Colonel Robert D. Heinl Jr., "The Collapse of the Armed Forces," *Armed Forces Journal* (June 7, 1971), 30–37.

20. "Special Message to the Congress on Draft Reform" (April 23, 1970).

21. Sheila Nataraj Kirby et al., "Diversity and the Success of Entering Classes at the U.S. Service Academies," RAND National Defense Research Institute (Santa Monica, CA, 2010).

22. Charles C. Moskos and John Sibley Butler, *All That We Can Be: Black Leadership and Racial Integration the Army Way* (New York: Basic Books, 1997).

23. "Senate Confirms Powell," *New York Times* (September 23, 1989).

24. "The Arms for War and the Hope for Peace" (March 19, 1991), https://www.c-span.org/video/?17156–1/arms-war-hope-peace, accessed June 28, 1991.

25. "Military Retirement Ceremony Address" (September 30, 1993), https://www.americanrhetoric.com/speeches/colinpowellmilitary retirementspeech.htm, accessed July 6, 2020.

26. The quoted phrase is the title of Dean Acheson's 1969 memoir, which was awarded the Pulitzer Prize for History.

27. Maureen Dowd, "War Introduces a Tougher Bush to Nation," *New York Times* (March 2, 1991).

28. "Address to the Joint Session of the 107th Congress (September 20, 2001).

29. Some might argue that Condoleezza Rice, who served as national security adviser during George W. Bush's first term as president, played a substantial role in paving the way for the Iraq War. The available evidence suggests otherwise. White guys like Cheney and Rumsfeld did not take Rice seriously. She occupied a seat near the center of power, but, apart from propping up the president's self-confidence, she appears to have wielded little influence. Michael J. Mazarr, *Leap of Faith: Hubris, Negligence, and America's Greatest Foreign Policy Tragedy* (New York: PublicAffairs, 2019), 86.

30. Steven R. Weisman, "Airing of Powell's Misgivings Tests Cabinet Ties," *New York Times* (April 19, 2004).

31. For the canonical text of the Bush Doctrine, see the president's "Graduation Address at West Point" (June 1, 2002).

32. Robert Draper, "Colin Powell Still Wants Answers," *New York Times* (July 16, 2020).

33. "Speech at the United Nations" (February 5, 2003), https://www.c-span.org/video/?c4716794/user-clip-colin-powells-speech.

34. Steven R. Weisman, "Powell Calls His U.N. Speech a Lasting Blot on His Record," *New York Times* (September 9, 2005).

35. "Interview with Vice President Dick Cheney," *Meet the Press* (March 16, 2003).

36. For a breakdown of U.S. military deaths by race in the Iraq War, see Nese F. DeBruyne, "American War and Military Operations Casualties: Lists and Statistics," *Congressional Research Service* (April 26, 2017).

37. Matt Taibbi, "16 Years Later, How the Press That Sold the Iraq War Got Away with It," *Rolling Stone* (March 22, 2019).

38. Sarah Abruzzese, "Iraq War Brings Drop in Black Enlistees," *New York Times* (August 22, 2007).

39. Brent Budowsky, "Obama's Speech Opposing the Iraq War" (October 2, 2002), https://www.huffpost.com/entry/obamas-speech-opposing-th_b_90944, accessed July 4, 2020.
40. "Timeline: US Military Presence in Afghanistan," *Al-Jazeera* (September 8, 2019), https://www.aljazeera.com/news/2019/09/timeline-military-presence-afghanistan-190908070831251.html, accessed July 5, 2020.
41. "Clinton on Qaddafi: 'We Came, We Saw, He Died,'" *CBS News* (October 20, 2011), https://www.cbsnews.com/news/clinton-on-qaddafi-we-came-we-saw-he-died/, accessed July 5, 2020.
42. "U.S. Strategic Nuclear Forces: Background, Developments, and Issues," *Congressional Research Service* (April 27, 2020).
43. "Text of President Obama's Speech in Hiroshima, Japan," *New York Times* (May 27, 2016).
44. Hans M. Kristensen and Matt Korda, "Status of World Nuclear Forces," *Federation of American Scientists* (April 2020).
45. For a narrative account, see Andrew J. Bacevich, *America's War for the Greater Middle East: A Military History* (New York: Penguin Random House, 2016).
46. "Full Replay/Transcript: Donald Trump Speaks in Greenville, NC" (September 6, 2016), https://www.realclearpolitics.com/video/2016/09/06/full_replaytranscript_donald_trump_speaks_in_greenville_nc.html, accessed July 6, 2020.
47. William H. Frey, "The US Will Become 'Minority White' in 2045, Census Projects," Brookings Institution (March 14, 2018).

7: KISSING YOUR EMPIRE GOODBYE

1. "Our Irish Regiments in the First World War," https://www.royal-irish.com/stories/our-irish-regiments-in-the-first-world-war, accessed July 15, 2020.
2. A Report to the National Security Council, "United States Objectives and Programs for National Security" (April 14, 1950).
3. "Address to the Democratic National Convention" (July 13, 1972), https://www.youtube.com/watch?v=BSNSVtFC-ZA, accessed July 18, 2020.
4. "A New Covenant for American Security" (December 12, 1991).
5. "Clinton's Words on Somalia: 'The Responsibilities of American Leadership,'" *New York Times* (October 8, 1993).

6. Donatella Lorch, "Last of the U.S. Troops Leave Somalia; What Began as a Mission of Mercy Closes with Little Ceremony," *New York Times* (March 26, 1994).

7. For a brief narrative account of the Somalia intervention, see Andrew J. Bacevich, *America's War for the Greater Middle East: A Military History* (New York: Penguin Random House, 2016), chap. 8.

8. See Bacevich, *America's War for the Greater Middle East*, chap. 10, for details.

9. In 2020, an international criminal court indicted Kosovo's president, Hashim Thaçi, for having committed war crimes. During the war, Thaçi had commanded the Kosovo Liberation Army, which the State Department classified as a terrorist organization. Peter Kingsley and Gerry Mullany, "Kosovo President Is Indicted for War Crimes for Role in War with Serbia," *New York Times* (June 24, 2020).

10. "Address on the Kosovo Agreement" (June 10, 1999).

11. Howard Fineman, "A President Finds His True Voice," *Newsweek* (September 24, 2001).

12. "Splitting the Check: When Allies Helped Pay for Middle East War," *NBC News* (September 14, 2014), https://www.nbcnews.com/storyline/isis-terror/splitting-check-when-allies-helped-pay-middle-east-war-n203756, accessed July 28, 2020.

13. Neta Crawford, "United States Budgetary Costs and Obligations of Post-9/11 Wars Through FY2020: $6.4 Trillion," *Costs of War Project* (November 13, 2019).

14. U.S. Treasury, "Historical Debt Outstanding—Annual 2000—2019" (n.d.), https://www.treasurydirect.gov/govt/reports/pd/histdebt/histdebt_histo5.htm, accessed July 28, 2020; Congressional Budget Office, "CBO's Current Projections of Output, Employment, and Interest Rates and a Preliminary Look at Federal Deficits for 2020 and 2021" (April 24, 2020), https://www.cbo.gov/publication/56335, accessed July 28, 2020.

15. William D. Lastrapes, "Why the $22 Trillion National Debt Doesn't Matter—Here's What You Should Worry About Instead," *Conversation* (February 14, 2019).

16. Peter S. Goodman, "The Dollar Is Still King. How (in the World) Did That Happen?," *New York Times* (February 22, 2019).

17. Veta Chan, "'There Are Plenty of Alternatives': The Pandemic Is Threatening to Dethrone the U.S. Dollar," *Fortune* (July 23, 2020).

18. U.S. Treasury, "Interest Expense on the Debt Outstanding" (June 4, 2020), https://www.treasurydirect.gov/govt/reports/ir/ir_expense .htm, accessed July 28, 2020; National Institutes of Health, "Budget" (June 29, 2020), https://www.nih.gov/about-nih/what-we -do/budget, accessed July 28, 2020.

19. Hillary Clinton, "American Global Leadership at the Center for American Progress" (October 12, 2011).

8: THE HISTORY THAT MATTERS

1. T. S. Eliot, "Little Gidding" (September 1942).

2. "Reports that say that something hasn't happened are always interesting to me, because as we know, there are known knowns; there are things we know we know. We also know there are known unknowns; that is to say we know there are some things we do not know. But there are also unknown unknowns—the ones we don't know we don't know. And if one looks throughout the history of our country and other free countries, it is the latter category that tend to be the difficult ones." "DoD News Briefing—Secretary Rumsfeld and Gen. Myers" (February 12, 2002).

3. "War Message to Congress" (April 2, 1917).

4. For a readily available example by a leading revisionist, see Harry Elmer Barnes, *The Genesis of the World War: An Introduction to the Problem of War Guilt* (New York: Alfred A. Knopf, 1927). In the preface, Barnes writes, "Never was any previous war so widely proclaimed to have been necessary in its origins, holy in its nature, and just, moderate and constructive in its aims. Never was a conflict further removed in the actualities of the case from such pretensions." The entire book is online at https://archive.org/stream/genesisofworldwa00harr /genesisofworldwa00harr_djvu.txt.

5. Robert A. Divine, *Second Chance: The Triumph of Internationalism in America During World War II* (New York: Atheneum, 1967).

6. For video see https://www.youtube.com/watch?v=OQwdyzkDjdA. The narrator, David McCullough, says of this first meeting between the American president and the British prime minister, "The course of the war would be determined by the convergence of these two extraordinary personalities." Stalin might have entertained a different view.

7. The point of origin for this project is William Appleman Williams, *The Tragedy of American Diplomacy* (Cleveland: World Publishing Company, 1959), with subsequent revisions.

8. In a 1954 letter to the executive secretary of the American Historical Association, the influential historian–political operative Arthur Schlesinger Jr. went so far as to denounce Williams as a "pro-communist scholar." Paul Buhle and Edward Rice-Maximin, *William Appleman Williams: The Tragedy of Empire* (New York: Psychology Press, 1995), 95. By 1966, Schlesinger had had enough, declaring it time to "blow the whistle before the current outburst of revisionism regarding the origins of the cold war goes much further." Schlesinger, letter to the editor, *New York Review of Books* (October 20, 1966).

9. Francis Fukuyama, "The End of History?," *National Interest* (Summer 1989).

10. Bill Clinton, "New Dimensions for American Security," speech delivered at the Foreign Policy Association, New York (April 1, 1992).

11. Eliot A. Cohen, "This Is World War IV," *Wall Street Journal* (November 20, 2001); Norman Podhoretz, *World War IV: The Long Struggle Against Islamofascism* (New York: Doubleday, 2007).

12. The authoritative archive of the 1619 Project is at https://www .nytimes.com/interactive/2019/08/14/magazine/1619-america -slavery.html?searchResultPosition=1, accessed August 11, 2020.

13. "Unite the Right Rally," https://en.wikipedia.org/wiki/Unite_the _Right_rally, accessed August 13, 2020.

14. Robin Pogrebin, "Roosevelt Statue to Be Removed from Museum of Natural History," *New York Times* (June 21, 2020).

15. Steven Greenhut, "'Cancel Culture' Is a Dangerous, Totalitarian Trend," *Reason* (August 7, 2020).

16. See, for example, the famous "Harper's Letter," signed by dozens of American writers and intellectuals. "A Letter on Justice and Open Debate," *Harper's* (October 2020).

17. "Transcript: Joe Biden's DNC speech" (August 21, 2020), https:// www.cnn.com/2020/08/20/politics/biden-dnc-speech-transcript /index.html, accessed September 28, 2020.

CONCLUSION

1. Leon Wieseltier, "Hitler Is Dead," *New Republic* (May 27, 2002).
2. Wieseltier's piece elicited fierce denunciations in return. See, for example, Ron Rosenbaum, "Can Wieseltier, D.C.'s Big Mullah, Have It Both Ways?," *Observer* (June 10, 2002).
3. A representative work is Lawrence F. Kaplan and William Kristol, *The War over Iraq: Saddam's Tyranny and America's Mission* (San Francisco: Encounter Books, 2003).
4. Harry S. Truman, *Memoirs* (Garden City, NY: Doubleday, 1956), vol. 2, 332–33; Lyndon Johnson, "The President's Address at Johns Hopkins University: Peace Without Conquest" (April 7, 1965).
5. A sampler: Eugene Scott, "Dick and Liz Cheney Liken Iran Deal to Munich Pact," CNN.com (August 29, 2015); Al Weaver, "Graham: Obama Is Worse Than Neville Chamberlain," *Washington Examiner* (September 10, 2015).
6. "President Macron's Initiative for Europe: A Sovereign, United, Democratic Europe," Ministry of European and Foreign Affairs (n.d. [2020]).
7. "Number of Deaths from Terrorist Attacks, World, 1970 to 2017," *Our World in Data*, https://ourworldindata.org/grapher/deaths-from-terrorist-attacks, accessed August 18, 2020.
8. On August 18, 2020, a web search using the terms "terrorism" and "there is no military solution" yielded 365,000 hits.
9. For a primer, see the *Global Exchange* (Issue 3, 2018). This publication of the Canadian Global Affairs Institute contains several articles on Arctic sovereignty.
10. For a concise description of Mexico's security problems, see Carlos Galina, "Mexico's Security Dilemma," Council on Foreign Relations (January 14, 2020).
11. The data come from readily available agency websites.
12. Jim McKay, "A Depleted Strategic National Stockpile in a Time of Need," *Emergency Management* (May 7, 2020).
13. David Thornton, "Coast Guard Needs More Money to Address Aging Fleets, Readiness," *Federal News Network* (June 5, 2019).
14. On the projected cost of the B-21 bomber, see Ellen Ioanes, "The US Air Force's Secretive New B-21 Stealth Bomber Will Take to

the Skies Soon," *Business Insider* (July 24, 2019); on the inadequacy of the Forest Service's tanker fleet, see Bill Gabbert, "Forest Service Needs to Be More Transparent While Spending Hundreds of Millions Contracting for Firefighting Aircraft," *Fire Aviation* (June 2, 2020).

ACKNOWLEDGMENTS

I began *After the Apocalypse* in March 2020 and finished in October, just a few months more than it took Marc Bloch to write *Strange Defeat*. Throughout most of that period, libraries were closed, obliging me to rely on whatever materials I had on hand and those I could purchase plus, of course, the internet. A book written on this subject in more favorable circumstances would no doubt have allowed access to a wider range of research materials. But I doubt that those would have substantively affected my conclusions.

Before I began writing, I consulted various friends and colleagues about the proposed project's feasibility. Casey Brower, Mike Desch, Zach Fredman, Chas Freeman, Stephen Kinzer, Jim Kurth, Jackson Lears, Walter McDougall, Tom Meany, Paul Miles, Samuel Moyn, and Stephen Wertheim all offered advice and counsel for which I am very grateful. Whether they will agree with the result I cannot say, but I know that their contribution to the final result is immeasurable.

Neta Crawford, Matthew Petti, and Barrye Price weighed in with some key data. Lawrence Kaplan and David Warsh offered wise editorial counsel. Steve Brown, a dear friend ever since cadet days, reviewed the entire manuscript and removed innumerable infelicities.

My debt to my agent John Wright, my publisher Sara Bershtel, and my editor Tom Engelhardt can hardly be overstated. Thanks also to Hannah Campbell for efficiently presiding over the entire process of editing and producing the final book.

As for my darling Nancy, we have now been married more than fifty years. She remains the light of my life.

I have dedicated this book to two West Point classmates who died far too soon. In the army and after, Lonnie Adams and Doug Fitzgerald embodied the values that matter most: honor, courage, decency, and generosity of spirit. I miss them both more than I can say.

INDEX

ascent to White House, 2
books about, 69–70
demise of New Order, 21
on disappearance of COVID-19, 22
election to presidency in 2016, 26
foreign policy, 146
idiotic prognostications, 144
improvisation bordering, 21
malevolent presence of, 30
Niebuhr agreement with, 28
oust from White House, 158
presidency of, 1, 13–14, 107, 157, 158
promotion of hydroxychloroquine, 74
redeem America First, efforts to, 153
rise of, 19
uncontested Republican nomination
    of, 164
in United Nations General
    Assembly in 2017, 49
U.S.-Israeli relationship, 66–67
victory of, 127–28
Turkey, 48
Twain, Mark, 14, 15

Ukraine, 169
United Nations Security Council, 35,
    42, 63, 120
    Iraq into compliance with, efforts to
        bring, 121
United States
    air attacks in South Asia, 25
    air campaign against Serbia, 39
    China, relationship with, 53–56
    collaborative relationships, 49
    entry into World War I, 32
    Great Britain, relationship with,
        56–62
    involvement in killing of
        noncombatants, 24
    Israel, relationship with, 56–57,
        62–68
    military preeminence, 20
    ministrations, beneficiaries of, 23
    narrative abroad, 22–23
    New World, 32
    post–Cold War, 10, 21
    post–World War II era, 20

repositioning, 10
strongest military, 16
tradition of imperialism, 23
Warsaw Pact and, 50
See also U.S. policy
United States Africa Command
    (AFRICOM), 167, 168
United States Central Command
    (CENTCOM), 167, 168
United States European Command
    (EUCOM), 167, 168
United States Information Agency, 88
U.S. Coast Guard, 169
U.S. forces, 24, 126–27
    in Afghanistan and Iraq, 74
    encountered rebellious Filipino
        nationalists, 76
    expulsion from Arabian Peninsula, 6
    frenetic activity of, 100
    funding, 94
    sent to Persian Gulf, 117
U.S.-Iranian relations, 24
U.S.-Israeli relationship, 56–57,
    62–68
    defence ties, 63–66
    economic support to Israel, 65–66
    Israeli willingness to indulge U.S.
        policy, 64–65
U.S. policy, 50–51, 97
    American Exceptionalism, 5
    during Cold War, 125
    foreign policy, 44, 146
    global policy, 128
    invaded Iraq in 2003, 141
    national security policy, 10
    nuclear arsenal, 26
    Open Door policy, 53–65
    post 9/11, 3–4
    shaping, 26–27
    substructure of existing, 9
    See also United States
U.S. Senate Committee on Energy and
    Natural Resources, 91
The U.S. Army in the Iraq War, 69, 81

Victoria, Queen, 60
Viet Cong, 87, 89

ABOUT THE AUTHOR

ANDREW BACEVICH GREW up in Indiana, graduated from West Point and Princeton, served in the army, became an academic, and is now a writer. He is the author, coauthor, or editor of more than a dozen books, among them *The New American Militarism*, *The Limits of Power*, *Washington Rules*, *America's War for the Greater Middle East*, and *The Age of Illusions: How America Squandered Its Cold War Victory*. He is also cofounder of the Quincy Institute for Responsible Statecraft, a Washington think tank. Bacevich and his wife, Nancy, live with their dog, Buddy, in Walpole, Massachusetts.